Recipes
from

# Rome

## Praise for *Venice: Recipes Lost and Found* by Katie and Giancarlo Caldesi

'Part love letter to the Italian city, part recipe book, *Venice: Recipes Lost and Found* includes tantalising recipes from the husband-and-wife team.'

**RACHEL KHOO, DAILY MAIL**

◆◆◆◆◆◆◆◆

'The anecdotes and ingredients alike bring Venice right to your kitchen table with gusto.'

**THE GUARDIAN**

◆◆◆◆◆◆◆◆

'The Caldesis' recipes provide a delightful whiff of Venetian culinary life.'

**TELEGRAPH MAGAZINE**

◆◆◆◆◆◆◆◆

'Katie and Giancarlo Caldesi have dodged the tourists and unearthed some of the most delicious and authentic recipes that the romantic, alluring city of Venice has to offer ... *Venice* is a beautiful cookbook.'

**CHEF MAGAZINE**

◆◆◆◆◆◆◆◆

'Katie and Giancarlo Caldesi have pushed the boat out (pardon the pun) ... to find the most authentic – and delicious – Venetian recipes ... try everything and gawp at the gorgeous photography. '

**ITALIA MAGAZINE**

*Hardie Grant*

BOOKS

Recipes
from

# Rome

**Katie and Giancarlo Caldesi**
**Photography by Helen Cathcart**

# *Welcome to our compilation album*

This is how we have come to feel about the recipes in Rome. We have read modern-day blogs and ancient Roman scripts. We've talked to young and old Romans alike, and Giancarlo has been retracing his steps and friends since his days there as a waiter. We've visited the Eternal City many times and scoured Roman history books. Then we have collected together our findings into this collection of recipes.

We like to think of it as Rome's greatest hits but, as with the best of this sort of album, there are some surprise tracks along the way. So we have included the ever-popular *Carbonara* (see page 132), golden oldies such as the Roman-style veal *Saltimbocca alla Romana* (see page 197) and the very eighties Tiramisu (see pages 220–23). Some recipes are even more ancient, recreating how Julius Caesar would have entertained over 2,000 years ago.

We have done our own cover versions, like our new version of a spicy Cheese and Pepper Pasta, *Cacio e Pepe* (see page 134), and we have collaborated with some of the best chefs in Rome today, 'sampling' some of their recipes into our new versions. There are family favourites from our friend and busy mum Stefania Menichetti, who works every day and cooks brilliantly simple meals from just three ingredients for her family each night. We've included some soulful melodies, which originated during horribly tough times in the Jewish ghettos, where love triumphed over hate and Jewish mothers cooked comforting food for their families using what they had.

There are slow numbers, those that take time to develop their flavours, like the Oxtail Stew, *Coda alla Vaccinara* (see page 184), and seasonal hits such as *Vignarola* (see page 102), a spring vegetable stew, which appears fleetingly just once a year when fresh artichokes, broad (fava) beans and peas are available. And we have included the new kids on the block, young chefs who've created fiery numbers, such as the Red Pepper Sorbet (see page 57), whose colour and heat reflect the city.

It's taken a while to get under the skin of Rome. Perhaps because it is so big and bustling, and there is so much history spanning many centuries that dates, emperors, invasions and battles come and go; maybe it is just too much to take in. However, there is something special about Roman food that really makes it stand out from other regions. To define it better we asked Roman chefs and cooks to sum up their food; nearly all of them answered '*e vero*'. 'It is true'. We asked our Italian English-speaking friends what they meant by this because, really, could you not say this about all food? Perhaps a better translation would be 'honest' or 'simple' they said, but even these words are too humble to describe the layers of history and culture that have combined with local ingredients to produce this unique cuisine.

Then we realised what it is that we have come to love about Roman cooking: it is not afraid to be slapped on a plate. It doesn't need to hide under a garnish. There's no need for fancy presentation. It is in-your-face poor man's cooking, which hasn't changed for years. It is gutsy, no-fuss, no-frills cooking with an almost aggressive punch of flavour, which, once tasted, leaves you begging for more.

But what is it that makes Roman food like this? What are its origins and influences? What new recipes and ingredients did the many travellers to Rome bring with them? We have identified ten points that we consider have made Rome's culinary landscape what it is today.

Geographically, we kept our search to the centre, in an area you can walk around easily. There are many suburbs worth visiting, if time allows, but we were there to concentrate on the food you can find now and what went on in the past to make it what it is today.

# 01
# The food of the Roman Empire

It is hard to believe the area Rome inhabits once consisted of a festering pit of mosquito-ridden swamps around a river, seven hills and some huts lived in by shepherds. That was in the 9th century BC and, incredibly, within a thousand years this undesirable landscape had become the centre of the enormous Roman Empire. The swamps were drained, crops were grown in the volcanic soil, aqueducts brought fresh water, roads were laid, houses and even takeaway food counters were constructed, and the population rose to around one million inhabitants – a massive number at that time.

One of those million was the huge and bombastic character Marcus Gavius Apicius, who is widely thought to have written a cookbook entitled *Apicius: De re Coquinaria, 'Apicius: Of Culinary Matters'*. It is Europe's oldest surviving recipe book and its English translation is still in print today. Along with Marcus Gavius Apicius, there seem to have been two other men who could have written this collection of recipes any time between the 1st and early 5th centuries AD. However, Marcus Gavius Apicius was certainly a cook and recipe collector, and he enjoyed a lifetime of excess in terms of wealth and lavish food. He loved to indulge in rare and expensive foods from gourmet suppliers, such as a sauce made from mullet livers, truffles and exotic spices, which perhaps lead to his downfall. When he got down to the equivalent of his last million, he chose to kill himself rather than eat with the plebs and shop at the Roman equivalent of a

supermarket. (A pleb or plebeian, by the way, was anyone who was not a member of a small group of ultra-aristocratic families who claimed to go back to the founding of the city).

Key ancient flavours were spicy, sweet and sour; combinations made of fresh herbs, vinegar, honey and imported spices such as pepper, cumin, aniseed and coriander seeds. Many of these flavours were inspired by Greek cuisine. In fact, in *The Classical Cookbook* by Andrew Dalby and Sally Grainger they suggest that 'the Romans are said to have been "porridge-eating barbarians" before they discovered Greek food towards the end of the third century BC'. Sesame seed was a popular ingredient and there is evidence to show the ancient Romans also fried cannabis seeds. I particularly like the combination of honey and pepper; try the Roman Herb Salad dressing on page 32 and the *Globi* (Cheese and Honey Pastries) on page 69, they are surprisingly delicious.

In wealthy circles, food was seen as a source of entertainment and not merely fuel. It appears that the ancient Romans introduced the idea of dinner parties, salad dressings and sauces. Ready prepared sauces were available to buy much in the way we buy ketchup and soy sauce today. William Sitwell sums it up in his book *A History of Food in 100 Recipes*: 'At which point did Rome reach its zenith and what precisely symbolised that moment? ... Rome was at its peak when its sauces were at their best.'

*Garum*, a sauce probably a little like Marmite in that it was either loved or loathed, was strong, fishy

and used in abundance; it was shipped all over the Roman Empire. There were many different grades of it, so it was used by everybody, not just the wealthy. It was a liquid made from small fish guts mixed with salt that was left to ferment in the sun. Ray Laurence, a professor of Roman archaeology, suggests that the Romans knew about umami, which is reflected in their use of the strong savoury taste of *garum*. Often mixed with wine, vinegar or herbs, it was used to emphasise flavour rather like Worcestershire sauce or *nam pla* (fermented fish sauce). A similar delicacy called *colatura* is still made today in Cetara by the fishermen of the Amalfi Coast, and is used to beef up other sauces and also on its own on pasta. An unfermented and more accessible example of *garum* is Apicius's Hot Fish Pickle (see page 63); it is a spicy relish that is wonderful in salads or eaten with ricotta and Seeded Wine Crackers (see page 62).

One of the underlying drivers in ancient Roman cuisine seems to have been a desire for complexity: the more ingredients, especially spices that had travelled from exotic shores, the better to show your wealth and sophistication. It seems that they were not so much interested in taste as the sheer exoticism and difficulty of extracting the particular ingredient. Using it showed that you had the resources to acquire an array of fiddly ingredients, for example flamingos' tongues. (The flamingo itself was not exotic, but think of how much good flamingo meat must have been discarded when you killed them only for their tongues!)

# The Romans are said to have been porridge eating barbarians before they discovered Greek food towards the end of the third century BC

Like a PR campaign, it was a way of expressing Roman power over the known world. John Edwards, author of *The Roman Cookery Of Apicius*, makes the point that 'the secret of classical cookery is time', and certainly the upper classes had enough time and free labour to complete these arduous tasks. According to Pliny the Elder, foie gras was a Roman invention of the 1st century BC, and Apicius refers to the feeding of dried figs and sweet wine to hungry pigs to fatten their livers.

Due to the famous Trimalchio's feast scene in Petronius's *The Satyricon*, it is easy to assume that all the wealthy, or in this case nouveau-riche, ancient Romans ate excessive dinners most evenings. It is from this novel that we have the notion of them eating dormice covered in honey and sesame, larks' tongues, peacocks re-dressed in their feathers after cooking and raw eggs. It would have been a nasty, gluttonous assortment of badly matched food, like a Las Vegas all-you-can-eat buffet table with huge Romans wobbling off to vomit what they had eaten only to be able to start again. Trimalchio himself picks his teeth during the meal with a silver quill, takes a pee in public and talks openly about the state of his bowels.

However, although there were plenty of Romans who could afford debauched feasts like Trimalchio's and to behave like him, we can see from looking at other ancient Roman writers that many preferred to be virtuous and disciplined in their eating. For example, Marcus Porcius Cato, also known as Cato the Elder or Cato the Censor, was one of such people. It is from his book *On Agriculture*, his only book to have survived in its entirety, we have taken the marinated olive relish on page 66. We have also included the Sesame and Honey Biscuits (see page 214) and nut-filled *Ravioli Fritti* (see page 215) from the Greek rhetorician Athenaeus's book *Deipnosophistae*, or 'The Partying Professors', a captivating description of an imaginary dinner party, including gossip and debates. For an in-depth look at what the ordinary people of ancient Rome ate, see Mark Grant's fascinating book *Roman Cookery*.

Galen, a Greek doctor and philosopher, was interested in the diet of the poor. He believed the body had to have a balance of hot, cold, wet and dry, and of the four humours: blood, phlegm, yellow bile and black bile, which control pain and health. Galen believed that you should maintain the equilibrium of these states and bodily functions through food and drink. He ended up as the Emperor Marcus Aurelius's personal physician and wrote medical texts that were followed for centuries after.

By keeping the plebs fed, watered and entertained, Roman rulers kept its population happy for centuries until the fall of the Roman Empire in AD 476.

# 02
# Water

# 03
# Roman ingredients

'The best water,' the gentleman on the table next to us insisted, waving a bottle in his hand, 'was Acqua di Nepi.' His friends, however, disagreed. It seems that every Roman has a preferred spring to drink from, albeit via a bottle from source to table. Giancarlo remembers arguments with his friends over who had the best water in different areas of Rome; it affected the taste of the beloved pasta and the indispensable coffee. If you visit the Trevi Fountain, do admire the work of architects Salvi and Bracci, but also taste the water from a tap at the back of the fountain and think of its route. Originally the water flowed over 22 kilometres (13.5 miles) to get there and was initially brought into Rome mainly via underground channels dug by hand under the orders of ancient Roman statesman and architect Agrippa. After the aqueduct was destroyed in the Dark Ages – the period between the fall of the Roman Empire and the Renaissance – it was rebuilt during the Renaissance and later given due reverence by the construction of this tribute and fountain in 1762. As David Winner puts it in his book *Al Dente*, 'The true essence of old Rome, its pulsing heart, its throbbing lymphatic system, was its astounding network of aqueducts.' And on the water of the Trevi, 'The water here may, in fact, be the most remarkable on the planet. Into it is distilled the essence of the city's soul, its ancient laws, culture and philosophy.'

It seems to us that when writing a book on a particular region's cooking, the spirit of the place speaks to the writer, telling them how to approach it. In our first book, *Amalfi*, it was 'first, catch your fish', for our book on Venice it was 'first, take your pestle and mortar', and now for Rome it is 'first, grow your chillies, rosemary and mint on your windowsill'.

Originally, large Roman villas would have had their own herb gardens, but even now, when most Romans live in apartments, they grow the basic herbs in pots on their terraces. The ancients had a staggering range of herbs, including rue, rosemary, lovage, savory, thyme, spikenard, *pennyroyal*, *mentuccia* (lesser calamint), mint, basil and coriander (cilantro). Herbs were often used for medicine and the Romans had a vast array of herbal remedies, which they used to cure everything from coughs and headaches to more serious infectious diseases. Many of these herbs have since been shown as having genuine healing properties and are still used today either in their pure forms or as ingredients in more complex pharmaceutical drugs. Aloe vera, for example, was used by the Roman army to heal and soothe wounds, and today its ability to help treat minor abrasions, burns and some skin conditions is now widely accepted by the medical community. Garlic was believed to have health-giving properties, but to also attract scorpions and the strong smell was disapproved of by the wealthy.

These days garlic is acceptable, chillies have been welcomed since their arrival in the early 16th century and still the favourite herbs are rosemary, sage, parsley and *mentuccia*. Vinegar is splashed into cooking and anchovies are popped into dishes where you mightn't expect them, such as the Chickpea Soup on page 114, to pep up the flavour, just as they were two millennia ago. Two local sheep's cheeses – the salty, hard Pecorino Romano and *Pecorino Cacio de Roma*, the semi-soft cheese from Lazio – are almost worshipped and rightly so: do bring a large hunk back in your suitcase. Use it where you would use Parmigiano Reggiano or eat it on its own drizzled with mild honey. Enjoy the delicately flavoured fresh cow or tangy sheep's milk ricotta while you are there too, drizzled with honey for a breakfast treat or try it dolloped on to pasta (it looks quite messy but tastes amazing). For a staggering selection of Roman meats and cheeses go to the fine food store Volpetti in Testaccio.

# 04
# Roman
# Jewish food

Jews have gathered in Rome for more than 2,000 years, establishing the oldest Jewish settlement in Europe. Originally they came from Jerusalem in the 2nd century BC, as Rome was a centre of commerce and Jews were traders or they were prisoners of war brought to Rome and Spain as slaves. However, most Roman Jews are descendants of Jews who fled southern Italy during the Spanish Inquisition in 1492. It was from there they took with them many Arab cooking styles, such as the use of dried fruit and nuts, sugar, cinnamon, preserving techniques and recipes for ingredients such as artichokes and asparagus. Legendary food writer Claudia Roden told us that wherever in the world you see the sweet and textural combination of raisins and pine nuts it is likely the Jews brought it there from Sicily. From here, too, came the idea of cooking small pieces of food in batter in hot oil. Many Jews became *friggitori*, cooks who prepared fried fish and vegetables, and sold them on the corners of the ghetto to passers-by. The sweet ricotta cake called *cassola* is thought to have originally been a Sicilian dessert, similar to Martino de Rossi's White Ginger Cheesecake on page 205 (see page 12 for more on Martino). Aubergines (eggplants) were brought to southern Italy by Arab settlers who, in turn, had brought them from India and, as aubergines were known as a Jewish vegetable in Italy, it was probably the Jews who brought them to Rome.

The huge influx of Jews fleeing Spanish rule into cities in Italy concerned those in power and resulted in the building of a ghetto for the Jews in Rome. (While a ghetto has come to mean generally a poor run-down area occupied by ethnic minorities, historically a ghetto was specifically an area within a city where Jews were forced to live.) The ghetto in Rome was the worst and most cramped of all in Italy. The people who lived there were the poorest and given the worst piece of land, which frequently flooded as it was close to the river. They were allowed to leave the ghetto at sunrise and had to be back by sundown, but all had to wear yellow hats with bells on to distinguish them. This segregation lasted until 1870 when the Kingdom of Italy was created and Jews were finally given equal rights as citizens. By the end of the ghettoisation there were between 7,000 and 9,000 Jews living in just a few blocks of houses and roads.

The smelly fish market of Portico d'Ottavia was on the edge of the ghetto and Jews could work there but were not allowed to buy certain fish. Large ones were intended for Christians and small ones were left for the Jews. Actually, these smaller fish, such as anchovies, are very good for you and are packed with omega oils. Their strong desirable flavour enhanced other poor ingredients and anchovies are now used all over Rome. On one of our visits to what is now called the Jewish Quarter, we enjoyed a traditional layered 'pie' of bitter endive with fresh anchovies that when baked became both crisp and utterly moreish.

Micaela Pavoncello, our Roman Jewish guide around the ghetto, believes that the harsh conditions imposed on the Jews were supposed to break down their resolve so they would simply give up their religion. Even the position of the ghetto next to a convent was hoped to convince them to 'save their souls'. Paradoxically, it probably helped to preserve their identity; they refused to change and very much kept their traditions alive. Micaela says that still today, 'Every Passover, every Rosh Hashanah and every Shavuot every year, they eat the same thing.' Today, of the 16,000 Jews living in Rome, just 400 live in the ghetto, but older Jewish ladies still sit on the bench on the main street chatting away as they have done for centuries.

# 05
# The emergence of the renaissance

During the decline of the Roman Empire, Rome's aqueducts and grain supplies were destroyed by the barbarians, thereby cutting the lifeblood into the city. This brought Rome to a standstill and forced it into the Dark Ages, a period in time that was to last around a thousand years. The population dropped to around 50,000 who mainly lived near the river. Once more Rome became malarial and fell into ruins. The Forum – a collection of great buildings and structures that was used for public speaking, judicial proceedings, commerce and many other important aspects of Roman life, which made up the heart of ancient Rome – was dismantled and precious statuary was taken by the popes. The Circus Maximus, once one of the most respected buildings in Rome, became a market garden and home to lettuces, artichokes and vegetables rather than some of the Empire's best athletes.

It was only after Pope Sixtus IV was elected in 1471 that Rome was once again taken seriously by the north as he began to change the infrastructure of what would once again be a civilised city. He was able to spend huge amounts of money on paved roads, churches, bridges, the beginnings of the Trevi Fountain and the Vatican Library. He constructed the Ponte Sisto, which was the first bridge over the Tiber river since ancient times.

When the impoverished Signor and Signora Sacchi had baby Bartolomeo in 1421, in the small town of Piadena in Northern Italy, they couldn't have had any idea of the life he would lead or the effect he would have on Italy and the beginnings of the Renaissance. Bartolomeo became known as Platina, the Latin name for his birthplace. He was a humanist, a select group of men who were scholars of classical literature and grammar, poetry and moral philosophy. Humanists looked back to the art, architecture and sculpture of the ancients and it was their new way of thinking that was instrumental to the birth of the Renaissance.

Platina moved to Rome in 1462 and met Martino de Rossi, also known as Maestro Martino, a cook to a priest. Together they decided to create a book of Platina's thoughts on food and Martino's recipes. Martino had begun a cookbook on Renaissance food entitled *Libro de Arte Coquinaria*, 'The Art of Cooking', but with Platina's help his recipes would be translated into Latin (which gave it literary gravitas) and accompanied by Platina's musings on the nutritional and medical aspects of food in the first-ever printed cookbook *De Honesta Voluptate et Valetudine*, 'On Respectable Pleasure and Good Health'. Martino and Patina included listings of grand dishes from classical antiquity, such as peacocks re-dressed in their plumage, but they were also concerned with the source of their ingredients and favoured a certain delicacy and simplicity to their food. Lighter dishes such as quiche-style open tarts with a filling of cheese and spinach, and fish cooked with wine and herbs would begin a new phase of Renaissance cooking.

While he was writing *De Honesta Voluptate et Valetudine*, Platina was suspected of being involved in a plot to kill Pope Paul II, who subsequently threw him in jail. Platina and his friends were thought to be heretics and disliked by the church for their ideas. They were so fascinated by the ancient world that they even held toga parties. While in jail, Platina managed to continue writing despite being tortured on the rack and suffering damage to his right arm. Upon his release, Gonzaga, a nobleman and friend, took Platina in and helped with his recovery, and he finally finished the book. In it, Platina wrote a warning, among many other rules of eating, that one shouldn't consume too many melons after a full meal. Bizarrely, Pope Paul II died of eating too many melons. This left the way for the new Pope Sixtus IV who liked Platina and employed him as Vatican librarian. Platina finished the book ready for print in 1468.

# 06
# Sugar and spice and all things nice

Bartolomeo Scappi, born in Lombardy in 1500, would surely have approved of this nursery rhyme. During the 16th century he rose to fame by cooking outrageous banquets for the fabulously rich, including six popes, for two of whom he became private chef. When working for Cardinal Lorenzo Campeggio in 1536, to impress the Emperor Charles V, Scappi cooked a feast of 13 courses comprising 789 elaborate dishes. Preparing such feasts required not only incredible organisational skills, but also specially designed equipment; he had a cauldron that could hold 700 litres of water and had to be moved using chains and rope and four men.

Scappi took the role of chef very seriously and devoted his life to cookery. He never married or had children, but instead left his legacy in the form of a thousand recipes collated into a six-volume piece of work called simply *Opera* or '*Works*'. Through this you can see his vast knowledge of regional Italian dishes as well as those from other European and North African countries. He was among the first of the Renaissance cooks, which is demonstrated through his use of offal and some of his recipes that show a regard for simplicity of ingredients and flavour in imitation of ancient Roman cookery. Scappi also obviously had no budget to worry about: recipe 25 from '*Book III – Lean Dishes*' (to be enjoyed when meat was not allowed) of *Opera* calls for a pound of caviar – only to be made into an omelette and garnished with cinnamon, sugar and orange juice!

Many of Scappi's recipes are similar to one another, with perhaps one or two ingredients changing between them. There are more than 50 thick soups usually made with broth, or on lean days almond milk, one of which inspired the White Chicken and Almond Soup on page 104. Through his book we can see the introduction of butter and milk, and the beginnings of flaky pastry. Many of his promising-sounding savoury recipes end with a dusting of cinnamon and sugar, rendering the dish unpalatable to modern tastes but, nonetheless, there are plenty that sound delicious.

# 07
# The advent of modernity

From the 16th century spices were abandoned and the simple style of Italian cooking that we love so much today emerged: *la cucina semplice*. With better transportation, tomatoes, chilli and pasta became widely available and were adopted into all of the regions' cuisines. Food across the whole of Italy has hardly changed since. And it is unlikely to do so; saying that Italians are fiercely proud of their traditional dishes is an understatement.

As one of the great defenders of tradition, famous Roman food writer Ada Boni wrote *La Cucina Romana*, '*Roman Cuisine*', and *Italian Regional Cooking*. She lived from 1881 to 1973 and wanted to teach people to cook, namely the housewives of the day, so that they could continue Italy's cooking traditions and the recipes wouldn't be lost. She felt good food was central and crucial to a good life. As the title of her masterwork *The Talisman of Happiness* suggests, she was motivated by a desire to spread the joy of cooking and famously said, 'There can be no true happiness if such an essential part of our daily lives as eating is neglected. Cooking is the most cheerful of arts and the most pleasant of sciences.'

At so many points in recent history Italy has fought off attack from foreign intervention in food. Kebab shops are frowned upon by the older generation and, apart from the odd Chinese restaurant, the only alien food is sushi, perhaps because it too relies upon simplicity and fresh ingredients. The Slow Food Movement began in Rome in 1986 as a protest against McDonald's opening near the Spanish Steps and the overall globalisation of food, and it is now a worldwide movement.

*There can be no true happiness if such an essential part of our daily lives as eating is neglected. Cooking is the most cheerful of arts and the most pleasant of sciences.*

# 08
# The fifth quarter

Romans are carnivorous souls. The ancient Romans who could afford it ate all parts of the animal believing that offal made you strong (and actually they were right). 'Offal,' our friend Paolo Trancassini from the restaurant La Campana, told us, 'is like a blue blazer: it isn't ever in or out of fashion; it's a stable classic.' From 1890, Europe's largest slaughterhouse was in Testaccio and the workers were paid in part with a bag of offal known as *quinto quarto*, the 'fifth quarter'. It was made up of the least desirable parts that fetched the worst price. Ironically, today the traditional dishes made from offal are some of Rome's most celebrated and loved.

Cured meats such as *guanciale*, made from sweet and delicately flavoured pork cheeks, are used to flavour pasta dishes like carbonara and *amatriciana*. Locally made pancetta and prosciutto is widely available but a newcomer to the scene is *pata negra*, also called *jamón ibérico*, the Spanish ham that we were surprised to see in Rome's more fashionable restaurants.

*Offal is like a blue blazer: it isn't ever in or out of fashion; it's a stable classic.*

# 09
# City dwellers need quick fixes

Modern day Romans love to eat out and this seems to be a habit that has continued since ancient times when bars called *popinae* served fried fish such as mackerel, sausages, stews, bread and cheese. Hot food was served from a *thermopolium*, 'a warmed counter', the best example of which can be seen today in Pompeii. The modern *tavola calda*, an informal restaurant where food is self-service from a hot buffet, is a descendant of a *popina*. Many Roman houses didn't have kitchens until recent centuries and even now they are often small. Hence the need to eat out. Street food has existed in Rome for millennia.

At a *tavola calda*, as well as at a *trattoria* or *osteria*, inexpensive homely food such as the chicken *Cacciatora* on page 172 can be eaten, or *Supplì* (rice fritters) like the ones on page 96 can be bought from bars and small shops. Many restaurants have a daily changing menu with speciality dishes served on particular days such as chickpea soup on Tuesdays, '*gnocchi Giovedi*', which means 'gnocchi Thursdays', and *baccalà e ceci*, salt cod and chickpea stew, served on Fridays, so the locals can pick their day.

Thirty years ago most restaurants were *trattorie* that served good home cooking at very reasonable prices. La Campana owner Paolo told us that in the seventies you could only eat well in the centre of Rome when it was '*monumenti e tavoli*', or 'monuments and tables'. Today, he feels eating out has changed with tourism. Giancarlo thinks you can have the best and the worst plate of pasta here, but good food abounds if you know where to look and follow the locals.

# 10
# Escape the heat; head to the hills to eat roast pork

In summer, Rome is baking hot and Romans have for centuries gone to the surrounding hillside towns of Castelli Romani, Frascati, Ariccia, Albano and Rocca di Papa to enjoy the fresh breezes. It is here you will eat in a *fraschetta*, a restaurant where originally you brought your own food and they would sell you *frascati* wine made from grapes grown in the local volcanic soil. Nowadays, their speciality is roast pork – the famous *Porchetta*, see pages 166–69 for our recipe. This and the vast assortment of side dishes makes the trip more than worthwhile.

Roman food is completely tied to the past and the peoples who have passed through the Eternal City. It is the place, the sunshine and the terrain; it's all bound together and all part of the same thing. We went with every intention of seeking out the latest food trends in Italy's capital city but found very few. Tradition is served in heaps and, happily, it seems that is what the Romans want. ◆

# A few notes before we start cooking

### Rendered pork fat

In the past it was easier to use pork fat to cook rather than expensive olive oil. It has a higher smoke point than olive oil and imparts a subtle flavour to recipes that is reminiscent of the fried bread of Katie's childhood. Giancarlo remembers doing this in his youth, as when the olive oil had run out for the year, pork fat was the only alternative. We render down fatty cuts of pork such as bath chaps by cooking the chopped fat slowly over a gentle heat. When a pool of fat appears in the bottom of the pan, pour it off into a bowl and return the pan to the heat. Continue until no more fat appears from the pieces of pork. Allow the fat to cool, cover and chill in the fridge. It will keep for weeks, even months, and can be spooned out as you need it.

### Herb paste to begin meat dishes

Pork fat is often used to form the basis of a paste; finely chopped with rosemary, garlic and seasoning for example. This way it doesn't need to be rendered first. The back fat of pork known as *lardo* is ideal for this but it is very expensive so better to ask your butcher for offcuts of waxy fat that will break down easily, or use fatty streaky unsmoked bacon instead. Finely chop it into a paste with a large cook's knife on a board.

### Two qualities of extra-virgin olive oil

We always use extra-virgin olive oil for cooking and for dressing raw or cooked food. A more basic one is used for frying and we use a really good single-estate olive oil for dressing a salad, a hot steak or swirling over soup.

### Oven temperatures

All the oven temperatures given in Celsius and Fahrenheit are for a fan-assisted oven. If your oven doesn't have a fan, please adjust the temperature accordingly. Gas mark temperatures are for a standard non-fan gas oven.

# Antipasti & Vegetables

It seems incredible that if we could travel to Rome as it was 2,000 years ago, we could sit on a stool at a bar, sip chilled wine and eat bar snacks just as we could if we went there today. The flavours of some of the recipes we have unearthed from that time are as enjoyable to us now as they were to Romans then.

Vegetables have always been plentiful in the Roman diet, as well as cereals and pulses, because they are cheap and readily available. In ancient Rome they were made into purées, relishes and dips and eaten with bread or crackers. Vinegar and herbs were used to dress salads as olive oil was expensive. Vegetarianism, whether by choice or purse, was not unheard of; Roman chef and restaurant owner Arcangelo Dandini told us that the legionnaires ate a diet of pecorino, farro (a grain), almonds, fruit and dates, as they were easy to eat when marching, only eating meat once they had set up camp. We've read that they might have used their helmets to cook in, particularly *puls*, a porridge made from barley or farro. We are sceptical this was general practice though – imagine having to scrub burnt porridge off your helmet before you could put it on!

When the Romans settled in Britain they brought their taste for vegetables with them. They introduced us to garlic, rosemary, onions, shallots, celery, peas, asparagus, thyme, bay, basil, walnuts and chestnuts. They also encouraged the cultivation of dessert apples and mulberries, and introduced other fruits like grapes and cherries.

Today, vegetable dishes and antipasti pretty much merge into one, which is why we have kept our selection of historical and modern day dishes together in the same chapter. Vast arrays of vegetables are often simply steamed, fried or roasted and eaten as part of antipasti or ordered after the main course. Every time we visit Rome the selection changes, from artichokes and monk's beard – known as *agritti* – in early spring, to broad (fava) beans – *fave* in Roman – and the pointed green cauliflower called *romanesco* a little later, and locally grown strawberries in summer. Bitter greens such as *cicoria*, a member of the chicory family, are highly prized, as are porcini mushrooms, when in season.

PUNTARELLE CON SALSA DI ALICI

# Chicory with Anchovy Dressing

**SERVES 6** (as a starter)

Each winter Romans go crazy for this crisp salad drizzled with a piquant dressing made from anchovies, garlic and very good olive oil. Thin curls are made from the shoots of the tender heart of a variety of chicory known as *puntarelle* meaning 'little tips'. They are pushed lengthways through a metal mesh and the resulting lengths are soaked in water so that they curl up. *Puntarelle* are difficult to find outside Italy, but this wonderfully pungent dressing is also perfect for a salad of fennel, endive and lettuce.

### METHOD

Wash the *puntarelle* in cold water, and remove and discard the dark outer leaves. Cut the inner, more tender, pale green fingers into thin strips with a large cook's knife or, if you have one, push them through a *puntarelle* cutter. Discard any tough, stringy leaves. Soak in a large bowl of cold water for 15 minutes until they curl. Drain and set aside. If you are using endives instead, cut off and discard the base, then finely chop the leaves into long strips. Do the same with the fennel and cut the celery into thin slices, then add both to the endive (or *puntarelle*). Set aside.

Make the dressing by whizzing all the ingredients together in a food processor, or by finely chopping the anchovies and garlic together and then whisking them into the oil and vinegar in a bowl. Toss the *puntarelle*, or alternative vegetables, in a large bowl, then divide between 6 individual bowls and drizzle over the sauce.

### FOR THE SALAD

1 head *puntarelle* or 2 endives

1 fennel bulb

3 celery sticks

### FOR THE DRESSING

7 tinned anchovy fillets in oil

1 small garlic clove

8 tablespoons extra-virgin olive oil

1 tablespoon white wine vinegar

CARPACCIO DI MANZO CON SALSA DI SENAPE E LIMONE

# Carpaccio of Marinated Beef with a Mustard and Lemon Dressing

**SERVES 10–12** (as antipasti or a starter)

At the elegant Pierluigi restaurant in the heart of Rome, Roberto, the owner, makes his version of beef carpaccio. He cures beef fillet overnight with vinegar and lemon, then slices it finely and serves it splashed with mustard sauce. The wafer-thin slices melt on your tongue; We could eat this all day with a chilled tall glass of *bollicine*, 'little bubbles'. Happy days.

### METHOD

Make the marinade by mixing everything together in a large bowl, then pour it into a suitably sized container that will fit the fillet and also inside your fridge. Season the fillet generously and then immerse it in the marinade in the container. Cover with baking parchment or a lid and refrigerate for 24 hours.

Mix the dressing ingredients together in a lidded jar and shake well to combine. Taste and adjust the seasoning as necessary. Remove the beef from the marinade and pat it dry with kitchen paper. Using a sharp knife, cut the fillet into very fine slices, or use a meat slicer if you have one. This is easier to do if the fillet is chilled in the freezer for 30 minutes first.

Arrange the carpaccio on a plate with the rocket and serve splashed with the dressing. Any uncut fillet can be wrapped, frozen and used within 3 months.

1 x 1 kg (2lb 3 oz) beef fillet, trimmed of any fat

Fine salt and freshly ground black pepper

Handful of rocket

### FOR THE MARINADE

500 ml (17 fl oz) water

500 ml (17 fl oz) white wine

500 ml (17 fl oz) white wine vinegar

Juice of 2 lemons

### FOR THE DRESSING

5 tablespoons extra-virgin olive oil

1 tablespoon lemon juice

2 teaspoons Dijon mustard

Salt, to taste

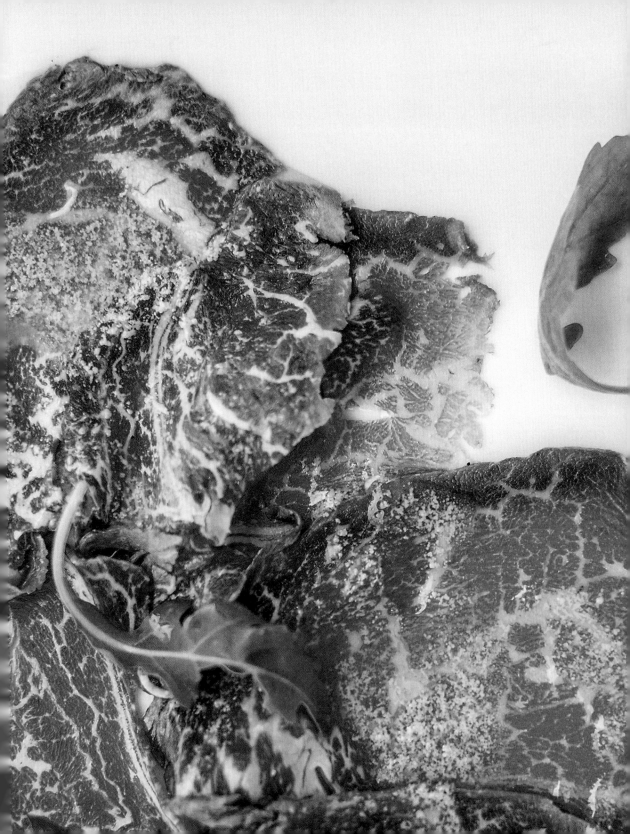

POMODORI RIPIENI O INSALATA DI RISO

# Stuffed Tomatoes or Rice Salad

**SERVES 6** (as antipasti or a side dish)

Stuffed tomatoes are often served as part of antipasti but they are also great as a vegetable side dish with grilled meats. When I was making these I left a bowl of the filling on the side while emptying out the tomatoes; our son Flavio (ever the hungry teenager) ate it and proclaimed it the most delicious rice salad. Although I wasn't amused as I had to make the stuffing all over again, I was pleased that he had discovered the recipe had a dual purpose, hence the name of the dish. If you are making it as a rice salad double the quantity to serve four. You don't need the tomatoes and you can keep or omit the cheese as you wish; I prefer it without and Flavio loves it with. And you can add a tin of tuna or sardines to bump it up into a main course.

**METHOD**

Heat the oven to 200°C (400°F/ Gas 7) if you are making the stuffed tomatoes. Put the rice into a saucepan with the hot stock or water and add a little salt. Bring to the boil, then reduce the heat to medium and cook the rice until just soft; this should take around 15 minutes. Drain, then wash briefly with cold water to separate the grains and cool the rice down. Set aside.

Halve the tomatoes around the equator and not pole to pole. Leaving the outer flesh intact, scoop out the seeds and central fleshy part of each tomato with a teaspoon (I use a serrated grapefruit spoon for this) and put it into a sieve over a bowl to collect the juice for use later. Using your finger, wipe the inside of the scooped out tomatoes with a little salt to season them. This will also help the water come out from them. Stand the tomato halves cut side down on a rack or tray to drain out the excess water while you make the stuffing.

Heat the oil in a frying pan and fry the onion over a gentle heat for about 5 minutes until just softened. Add the garlic and fry for another minute. Pour into a large bowl and add the cooled cooked rice and the rest of the ingredients, mixing to combine. Stir in around 5 tablespoons of the reserved strained tomato juice. Taste and season as necessary. This can now be served as a rice salad.

To continue with making the stuffed tomatoes, divide the rice filling between the tomato shells and drizzle a little olive oil over each one. Put them on a baking tray; if they don't stand up on their own cut a little sliver off the bottom to flatten it out, but make sure you don't make a hole all the way through. Bake for between 15–20 minutes until lightly browned and just on the point of collapse. Don't push your luck or they will fall apart. Remove from the oven and serve straight away or allow to cool to room temperature.

100 g (3½ oz/scant ½ cup) arborio rice

400 ml (13½ fl oz) hot homemade chicken stock (see page 107) or water

600 g (1 lb 5 oz) medium tomatoes or at least 6 (omit these for the rice salad)

2 tablespoons olive oil, plus extra for drizzling

1 medium white onion, finely chopped

1 fat garlic clove, finely chopped

4 tinned anchovy fillets in oil

2 tablespoons sultanas, soaked in a little water for 30 minutes

25 g (1 oz) pine nuts

4 heaped tablespoons flat-leaf parsley, finely chopped

1 heaped teaspoon dried oregano

50 g (2 oz) Parmesan

Salt and freshly ground black pepper

CARCIOFI ALLA ROMANA

# Roman Artichokes with Mint

**SERVES 6** (as a starter)

The Romans use *mentuccia*, a mint with small furry leaves that we call lesser calamint, but other types of mint will work equally well. This recipe first appeared in my book *The Italian Cookery Course* and was given to me by Gino Borella who worked as a chef in Rome for many years. Gino's cooking is always rich and full of flavour so I see no reason to alter his recipe now.

### METHOD

First clean and prepare the artichokes. Begin by pulling off the tough outer leaves; be brutal when removing them as tough leaves won't break down during cooking and you want the artichokes to be soft throughout. Trim the remaining leaves with a sharp knife, cutting roughly a third off the top. (You can do this with a sharp paring knife.) Cut the end off the stalk leaving approximately 5 cm (2 in) of stalk still on the artichoke. Cut away the dark tough outer parts of the remaining bit of stalk, exposing the paler inner stalk, and slice off the base scales of the artichoke with a knife. If the artichokes are young, and they should be, there shouldn't be a fluffy choke inside, but if there is remove it with a spoon.

In a small bowl, mix together the garlic, mint and parsley, and stuff the mixture into the artichoke centres. Get a lidded saucepan just big enough to snugly hold all the artichokes in when they're stood up in the pan with the heads down and stalks sticking up. You want the artichokes to be quite closely packed together when you add them to the pan, so that they won't fall over while cooking. Place the saucepan over a medium heat and add the olive oil. Gently place the artichokes in the pan, heads down and stalks up.

Pour in the water and if you have any leftover herbs you can add these too. Cover with a lid and leave to cook at a simmer for 45 minutes until tender. Shake the pan frequently to make sure they don't stick and add a little hot water if they look dry. Serve warm with the juices from the pan.

12 small artichokes

1 fat garlic clove, finely chopped

15 large mint leaves, finely chopped

Small handful of flat-leaf parsley (approx. 7g/¼ oz), finely chopped

3 tablespoon extra-virgin olive oil

100 ml (3½ fl oz) water

Salt and freshly ground black pepper

SPINACI SALTATI CON PINOLI E UVETTA SULTANINA

# Sautéed Spinach with Pine Nuts and Raisins

SERVES 6 (as a side)

Our Roman Jewish cookery teacher at our cookery school is Silvia Nacamulli. She loves to use the combination of pine nuts and raisins. The idea of putting dried fruit and nuts together in a recipe was introduced to the Jews by the Arabs when they lived alongside each other in Sicily for some eighteen centuries. We like to buy the soft juicy raisins that are ready to use. However, if they are dry soak them in a little hot water for ten minutes first.

## METHOD

Wash the spinach and, without completely draining it, put it in a deep saucepan with the salt. Cover and leave it to steam for 5–7 minutes until tender and wilted. Drain and leave to cool down. Squeeze the water out well, ideally with your hands. Roughly chop the squeezed spinach on a board with a large knife so it is easier to eat.

Heat the oil in a non-stick frying pan. Once the oil is hot, add the onion and season with a little salt and pepper. Cook over a low–medium heat, stirring occasionally, for 5–7 minutes until soft and starting to turn golden.

Add the steamed and squeezed spinach to the pan and stir it to combine with the onion. Sauté uncovered over medium heat for 10 minutes. Add the raisins and pine nuts, stir well and leave to sauté for a final 5 minutes. Serve warm or at room temperature.

1 kg (2 lb 3 oz) spinach leaves

1 tablespoon rock or coarse salt

4–5 tablespoons of extra-virgin olive oil

1 onion, finely chopped

Salt and freshly ground black pepper

3 tablespoons raisins

3 tablespoons pine nuts, toasted

CAVOLO NERO SALTATO CON PEPERONCINO E AGLIO

# Kale Sautéed with Garlic and Chilli

SERVES 4–6 (as a side)

Bowls of dark green chicory leaves, usually boiled then sautéed in garlic and chilli, are to be found in every restaurant in Rome. Romans love them and, though they have an acquired bitter taste, they do give you a certain self-satisfied feeling of eating something healthy; a 'you know you have had your greens and your mother would be pleased with you' sort of feeling. However, more widely available here, and more to my taste, are kale or spinach, either of which can be used for this recipe. The beautiful dark-leaved *cavolo nero*, or 'black kale', is becoming more common over here, when it is in season, but any kale is fine.

## METHOD

If using kale, remove and discard the entire length of the stalk that runs down the length of the leaf, so that you are left with just the soft parts of each leaf. Wash them under cold water. Very roughly chop the kale or spinach leaves and cook them in a steamer or large saucepan of salted boiling water for 7–10 minutes for kale and 2–3 minutes for spinach until just cooked. Drain and set aside.

Heat the oil in a large frying pan over a medium heat and, when hot, add the garlic, chilli, a generous pinch of salt and a good grind of pepper. Fry for about 2 minutes until the garlic and chilli soften, but watch they don't burn. Add the cooked kale or spinach and fry for around 5 minutes, stirring constantly, to ensure it is thoroughly coated in the chilli and garlic oil. If necessary, add a little more olive oil to stop it sticking. Transfer to a warmed dish and serve immediately.

1 bunch *cavolo nero* (black kale) or 1 kg (2 lb 3 oz) spinach leaves

3 tablespoons extra-virgin olive oil

2 garlic cloves, peeled and lightly crushed

½–1 red chilli, roughly sliced

Salt and freshly ground black pepper

PURÈ DI PATATE ALLE OLIVE

# Olive Mash

SERVES 8–10 (as a side)

Spoonfuls of buttery creamed potato studded with crushed olives make for a wicked change to everyday mash.

It is a perfect companion to stews, fish or offal. You can see a photo of the mash on page 183.

## METHOD

Put the unpeeled whole potatoes into a large pan of well-salted water and bring to the boil. Depending on the size of the potatoes, this can take up to 1 hour. They should be tender all the way through; a skewer should slide in easily when they are done. It may take a while to cook them like this, but the flavour is worth it. Italians will tell you that by keeping their skins on, the water doesn't penetrate through to the flesh so the potato doesn't become soggy and keeps it flavour. Drain and allow to cool for a few minutes, then peel.

Mash them using a potato ricer or food mill into a large bowl. Add the milk, cream, butter, salt and some generous twists of pepper. Use a hand-held blender to combine everything together and whisk in air and lightness; this will also help to get rid of any lumps so that the mash is completely smooth. Stir in the olives. Taste and adjust the seasoning as necessary.

To serve, form quenelles (elongated egg shapes) of the mash by taking a tablespoon of the mash and squeezing, smoothing and shaping it using a second tablespoon. Or simply serve in a warm serving dish.

1 kg (2 lb 3 oz) good mashing potatoes, such as Maris Piper

100 ml (3$\frac{1}{2}$ fl oz) whole (full-fat) milk

100 ml (3$\frac{1}{2}$ fl oz) double (heavy) cream

100 g (3$\frac{1}{2}$ oz) salted butter

1 teaspoon fine salt

Freshly ground black pepper

200 g (7 oz) whole black or green olives, pitted and quartered

PATATE ARROSTITE DELLA NONNA

# *Nonna's Potatoes*

SERVES 6 (as a side)

This is our friend Stefania's nonna's (grandmother's) recipe and it is now a family favourite; the potatoes are quick to prepare and become crispy outside and soft inside. Serve with simple chicken or fish dishes to allow all the flavours in the potatoes to shine. Stefania likes to fry them, but you can also roast them if you already have the oven on anyway – the difference is minimal.

METHOD

Heat the oven to 180°C (350°F/Gas 6) and line a baking tray with baking parchment, if roasting the potatoes. Cut the potatoes into 2–3 cm (³/4 – 1¹/4 in) cubes, leaving the skins on. Mix all of the ingredients together with the potatoes – including the oil if baking and omitting it if frying – in a large bowl and toss through.

To bake the potatoes, pour them on to the baking tray and bake for 20–25 minutes or until crispy and cooked through. If frying, heat the oil in a large non-stick frying pan and fry over a medium heat, tossing frequently, for about 20–25 minutes until browned and cooked through.

1 kg (2 lb 3 oz) potatoes, such as Desiree, King Edwards or new potatoes

1 red onion, coarsely chopped

1 sprig rosemary, cut into 4 pieces

2 teaspoons fennel seeds, lightly crushed in a pestle and mortar, or fresh fennel flower heads

4 bay leaves

6 sage leaves, each cut into 4 pieces

1 teaspoon dried oregano

2 garlic cloves, skins on and lightly crushed

Salt and freshly ground black pepper

5 tablespoons extra-virgin olive oil

INSALATA DI ERBE ALLA ROMANA

# Roman Herb Salad

**SERVES 6** (as a starter)

The ancient Romans used a huge variety of herbs in their food, which they either grew themselves or picked from the wild. Lovage, a herb similar to parsley but with a taste of celery, was widely available then and is easily grown now in a warm garden or on a windowsill. If you don't have it use its sibling, celery leaves; they have an equally peppery kick. This is a simple salad with a lovely dressing sweetened with chopped raisins and honey. It is perfect with fish, meat or boiled eggs.

### METHOD

Make the dressing by mixing the raisins, honey, vinegar and oil together in a large bowl, then season to taste. Toss all the salad ingredients together with the dressing and serve straight away.

FOR THE DRESSING

2 tablespoons raisins, finely chopped

2 teaspoons honey

2 tablespoons red wine vinegar

4 tablespoons good quality extra-virgin olive oil

Salt and freshly ground black pepper

FOR THE SALAD

1 head round lettuce or 2 baby gems, washed and roughly torn into pieces

Large handful of watercress, washed

$1/2$ cucumber, peeled, seeded and chopped into approx. 2 cm ($3/4$ in) cubes

2 tablespoons finely chopped lovage or celery leaves

10 large mint leaves, roughly chopped

Small handful of flat-leaf parsley, roughly chopped

INSALATA DI FARRO E PORRI CON PANCETTA E SPINACI

# Warm Farro Salad with Bacon, Leeks and Spinach

**SERVES 6** (as a side)

I absolutely love eating this dish. We cook it probably once a week and have it with scrambled eggs for breakfast, green salad and cold meats at lunch, and with sausages at supper (not all on the same day I hasten to add). I have suggested adding spinach or kale at the end and letting it cook in the heat of the pan, however this could easily be replaced by steamed broccoli florets or green beans, or left out altogether if you don't fancy adding anything. We eat variations of this dish through the year, adding baby spinach leaves from the garden in summer or chestnuts in winter, which make it quite a substantial dish. If you can't find farro, an ancient grain similar to wheat but lower in gluten, or you want a gluten-free alternative, use quinoa or brown rice instead.

## METHOD

Boil the farro in a saucepan of salted water or stock according to the packet instructions (usually around 12 minutes for quick-cook varieties and 30–40 minutes for whole farro) until soft to the bite.

Meanwhile, use a pair of scissors to cut the pancetta widthways into small strips around 1 cm (1/2 in) wide. Wash and top and tail the leek, then cut in half lengthways and chop finely. Heat the oil and butter in a large lidded frying pan over a medium heat and fry the bacon, leeks and rosemary gently for around 10 minutes until the bacon is cooked and the leek is soft. Remove from the heat and discard the rosemary.

Drain the farro and add to the pan with the bacon and leek. Stir in the spinach and chestnuts. Put the lid on the pan and put back over a low heat for about 5 minutes until the spinach has wilted and the chestnuts have warmed through. Season to taste and serve warm in winter or at room temperature in summer.

200 g (7 oz) farro
(quick cook or traditional)

1 litre (34 fl oz)
salted water, or ham
or chicken stock

4 rashers (slices) smoked
pancetta or streaky bacon

1 leek

4 tablespoons
extra-virgin olive oil

Knob of salted butter

1 sprig rosemary

2 large handfuls of spinach,
washed and shredded

100 g (3½ oz) chestnuts,
cooked and broken into
pieces (vacuum-packed
ones are ideal)

Salt and freshly ground
black pepper

VERDURE ALLA GRIGLIA

# *Barbecued Vegetables*

Everywhere there is a grill in use, vegetables are cooked over it. When I say grill, however, I mean an iron rack suspended over hot charcoal. A few Roman restaurants still incorporate this way of cooking into their kitchens and often they are on show to the customers. I seek out these restaurants as I really appreciate the flavour of grilling over wood. The flavour is wonderful and it is not the same as firing up a gas barbecue at all. Even in winter, I get our boys outside lighting up the fire and bringing charcoal to the white hot stage, which is perfect for cooking. Aubergine (eggplant), onion and courgette (zucchini) slices are grilled over the barbecue and served simply with sprinkling of marjoram or oregano, a little chopped garlic and parsley, and a splash of olive oil.

FAGIOLI CON LE COTICHE

# Slow-cooked Borlotti Beans with Tomatoes

**SERVES 6** (as a side)

Velvety soft beans are served in little terracotta bowls alongside roast pork in the hilltop town of Ariccia outside Rome. I asked for the recipe at the L'Aricciarola restaurant and was told the subtle porky flavour came from cooking the beans with a piece of pork skin and the use of pork fat in the cooking – a method not dissimilar to making Boston baked beans where the beans are cooked with a piece of pork belly, a recipe from thousands of miles away in the US. In fact, if your butcher can't supply you with a piece of pork skin, ask for a small strip of pork belly instead. The fat used to make the herb paste is usually firm white pork fat but fatty streaky bacon is an ideal substitute. Beans have been the staple diet of the poor for centuries and were also used to fill sacks in ancient Rome to cushion statues and monuments being shipped. You can see a photo of the beans on page 171.

2 fat garlic cloves

1 sprig rosemary, approx. 15 cm (6 in) long

5 sage leaves

Salt and freshly ground black pepper

100 g (3 1/2 oz) firm white pork fat or fatty streaky bacon

250 g (9 oz) borlotti beans, soaked overnight, or use 500 g (1 lb 2 oz) tinned borlotti beans

1 x 400 g (14 oz) tin plum tomatoes

2 level tablespoons tomato purée (paste)

1–1.3 litres (34–44 fl oz) vegetable, chicken or ham stock or water if using dried beans, or 500–600 ml (17–23 1/2 fl oz) vegetable, chicken or ham stock or water if using tinned beans

**FOR THE SOFFRITTO**

1 carrot

1 celery stick

1 medium white onion

3 tablespoons extra-virgin olive oil or rendered pork fat (see page 15)

100 g (3 1/2 oz) piece pork skin

2 bay leaves

**METHOD**

Using a large knife, finely chop the garlic with the leaves from the rosemary, the sage, some salt and pepper, and the pork fat or bacon together on a large board to make a herb paste. Finely dice the carrot, celery and onion to make a *soffritto*; either by hand or in a food processor.

Heat the herb paste in a large heavy-based saucepan and cook the *soffritto* with the oil or rendered pork fat, the pork skin and the bay leaves over a medium heat until soft. It will take around 15 minutes depending on the size of the vegetables.

Add the beans, tomatoes, purée and 1 litre (34 fl oz) of the stock or water for dried beans, or 500 ml (17 fl oz) if using tinned beans. Cook over a low heat for around 2 hours if using dried beans or 1 hour if using tinned until the beans are soft. Add a little more stock or water as necessary to ensure they do not dry out. Taste the beans when they are done and add more seasoning if necessary. Serve with crusty bread and the *Porchetta* on page 167, or any roast meat or sausages.

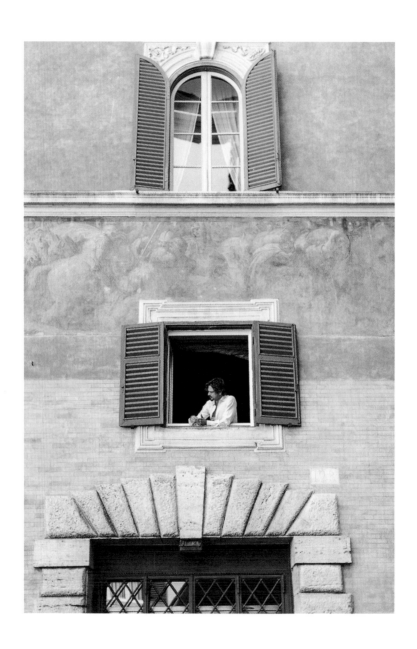

CIPOLLE SOTTO SALE

# *Salt-baked Onions*

**SERVES 6** (as a starter or side)

Whole onions baked in the fading embers of a fire until soft were a familiar sight to Giancarlo when he was growing up in rural Tuscany. With the recent rise in popularity of salt-baked vegetables the humble onion has undergone a transformation and now appears on the menus of some of the best restaurants in Rome. A slow-baked onion was the signature dish of famous Roman chef Salvatore Tassa. We discovered this version at Roscioli in Rome after one of the locals insisted we try them. Thank goodness they spoke out; we dunked toasted sourdough soldiers into a hollowed-out onion filled with a warm, cheesy, onion goo and never looked back.

I think this goes really well with the Slow-cooked Lamb on page 177, and can be done at same time as the lamb is cooking. Just give the onions another twenty minutes or so if you are doing this, as the oven will be at a lower temperature. These are also good on their own as a starter or as a vegetarian main course. Any colour of onions works but the shape is important: make sure that they are short and fat so that they can sit upright to hold the filling.

## METHOD

Heat the oven to 200°C (400°F/Gas 7). Pour the salt evenly into a large lasagne dish, and stand the onions (whole, with the skins still on) on the salt, roots-side down and tops pointing up. Cover the dish in foil, wrapping it right underneath so that it is well sealed, and bake for 1 hour. Remove the foil and continue to bake for another 30 minutes or until the skins have crisped and the onions feel soft when lightly squeezed (be careful not to burn yourself).

Remove the dish from the oven and transfer the onions to a plate to cool. Keep the baking dish of salt as you will need it again. Roughly cut off the top third of each onion, exposing the soft insides of the remaining two thirds. Scoop out the centre of each one with a spoon, putting the flesh into a bowl, leaving 2 layers of flesh and the base intact so that you have little onion bowls. If you spot a hole in the bottom of any, cover it with a small piece of the scooped-out onion. Also spoon out the flesh from inside of the cut-off tops and add to the bowl, but discard the skins.

Purée the scooped-out onion with the cheese and oil in a food processor; season to taste. Fill each of the onion shells with the mixture and then carefully transfer them back on top of the salt in the baking dish. Scatter each with a little more cheese and bake for about 15–20 minutes until browned and bubbling.

300 g (10 1/2 oz) coarse salt

6 medium brown or red onions

75 g (2 1/2 oz) Parmesan or pecorino, finely grated, plus extra to scatter

3 tablespoons extra-virgin olive oil

Fine salt and freshly ground black pepper

# *Green Beans with Lemon*

**SERVES 4** (as a side)

Dressed with a squeeze of lemon juice and good olive oil, long green beans are transformed into a simple warm salad. Italians seldom eat the beans squeaky and bright green, preferring them instead soft and dark green. They taste much better this way so we encourage you to cook them longer than usual and see the difference.

### METHOD

Steam or boil the beans in salted water for around 10–15 minutes; drain when tender and soft, rather than crunchy and squeaky. Transfer to a large bowl and splash on the lemon zest and juice, oil and seasoning. Toss gently to coat the beans in the dressing and taste; adjust the seasoning as necessary. Tip into a serving dish and serve hot or at room temperature.

250g (9oz) greenbeans

Finely grated zest of half a lemon

1 tablespoon lemon juice

2 tablespoons extra-virgin olive oil

Salt and freshly ground black pepper

CONCIA DI ZUCCHINE GRIGLIATE

# Grilled Courgette Salad

**SERVES 6** (as antipasti or a side)

You will often see 'concia', the name for this style of marinated courgette (zucchini) or aubergine (eggplant), written on menus, particularly in the Jewish area. It is thought that the recipe was brought to Rome by the Jews fleeing Sicily in the Spanish Inquisition. The courgettes are cut into circles or long strips and fried until brown, and then tossed with garlic, chilli and olive oil, turning bright green in colour as they cool down. They can be served at room temperature in a variety of ways: as a side dish to any meat or fish; stirred through cooked pasta with a handful of Parmesan and a splash of cream; as part of antipasti, usually with a sprinkling of vinegar and mint (this is called 'concia'); or added to a frittata with a little mint. Do deep fry them if you wish, but we prefer them grilled with light coating of seasoned olive oil. This method is suitable for slices of aubergine too, but you may need to give them a little longer under the grill. You can see a photo of this recipe overleaf.

## METHOD

Heat the grill to medium-high. In a bowl, toss the courgettes in 2 tablespoons of the oil along with some seasoning. Spread the courgettes on a baking tray in a single layer; you may need to do this in 2 batches. Grill until lightly browned, then turn the pieces over and brown the other side.

Meanwhile, combine the garlic, chilli (adjust the amount to suit your taste) and parsley in a bowl and stir in the remaining oil. When the courgettes are done, tip them into the bowl and gently toss through. Add the vinegar and mint at this point, if using. Allow the courgettes to cool to room temperature if you are serving them as an antipasti, or serve them warm as a side dish. Any leftovers can be stored in the fridge for 3 days, but don't serve them fridge cold when you come to use them

800 g (1 lb 12 oz) courgettes (zucchinis) (approx. 5 courgettes), cut into ½ cm (¼ in) thick slices

4 tablespoons extra-virgin olive oil

Salt and freshly ground black pepper

1 clove garlic, finely chopped

½–1 dried or fresh red chilli

2 tablespoons roughly chopped parsley

1 tablespoon red wine vinegar (optional)

1 tablespoon finely chopped mint (optional)

ZUCCA CON ROSMARINO E CUMINO

# Pumpkin with Rosemary and Cumin

SERVES 4 (as a side)

Rosemary grows wild in Italy, hence its use for centuries in cooking. Sweet and mildly spiced pumpkin marries perfectly with simply cooked fish, barbecued meats or roast peppers. This is based on an ancient Roman recipe made when cumin would have been much more precious and imported from Asia, possibly via Venice. You can see a photo of this recipe overleaf.

## METHOD

Heat the oven to 200°C (400°F/ Gas 7) and line a baking tray with baking parchment. Peel the pumpkin or squash and cut into wedges no thicker than 1 cm (1/2 in). Discard the seeds. Toss the pumpkin in a large bowl with the oil and salt and pepper until it is well coated. Pour the pumpkin on to the baking tray and roast in the oven for around 25–30 minutes until soft and lightly browned.

Meanwhile, melt the butter in a small saucepan over a medium heat and stir in the rosemary and cumin. Remove from the heat and set aside. Just before the pumpkin is ready, put a serving dish into the oven to warm – be careful it doesn't get too hot.

Tip the roasted pumpkin into the warm serving dish, pour over the spiced butter and serve warm.

## VARIATION

Cut the pumpkin into approx. 3 cm (1 in) cubes and steam or boil for 10–15 minutes until soft. Drain, if necessary, and transfer to a large bowl or the bowl of a food processor. Mash by hand or using your food processor with a dash of milk and a knob of butter to achieve a purée, then season to taste. Serve spooned on to a plate and topped with cooked white fish or steak, and drizzle over the warm rosemary and cumin butter.

1 pumpkin or butternut squash (approx. 700 g–1 kg / 1 lb 8 1/2 oz–2 lb 3 oz)

3 tablespoons extra-virgin olive oil

Salt and freshly ground black pepper

25 g (1 oz) salted butter

1 teaspoon rosemary leaves, finely chopped

1/2 teaspoon ground cumin

LENTILS IN RED WINE,
PAGE 44

PUMPKIN WITH
ROSEMARY & CUMIN,
PAGE 41

GRILLED
COURGETTE
SALAD,
PAGE 40

WILTED TOMATOES,
PAGE 44

LAGANOPHAKE

# Lentils in Red Wine

SERVES 4

This ancient dish is based on a recipe in Mark Grant's book *Roman Cookery*. I like to serve it with salads, boiled eggs or as an accompaniment to white fish. It also goes particularly well with the Fish and Bronze Fennel in a Parcel on page 151 or the Pumpkin with Rosemary and Cumin on page 41. See photo on previous page.

## METHOD

Fry the onion in the oil in a medium saucepan over a medium heat for around 10 minutes until soft. Add the lentils, cumin, thyme or oregano and aniseed, if using, and stir through. Pour in the wine and vinegar and cook for a few minutes, then add the stock or water. Bring to the boil and then reduce the heat to simmer. Cook, stirring occasionally, for around 45 minutes or until the lentils are soft. Just before serving, check the seasoning and add the dill and parsley.

1 onion, finely chopped

3 tablespoons extra-virgin olive oil

200 g (7 oz) Umbrian or puy lentils

1 teaspoon ground cumin

1/2 teaspoon thyme leaves or dried oregano

Pinch of ground aniseed (optional)

120 ml (4 fl oz) red wine

1 tablespoon red wine vinegar

700 ml (24 fl oz) vegetable or chicken stock (page 107) or water

1 tablespoon finely chopped dill fronds

Handful of flat-leaf parsley

Salt and freshly ground black pepper

POMODORI AL FORNO

# *Wilted Tomatoes*

**SERVES 6** (as a starter, side or antipasti)

In the heart of the old Jewish ghetto in Rome at La Taverna del Ghetto, we were served a plate of warm, sloppy, shrivelled tomatoes and a basket of bread. We can't say we were struck by the beauty of what lay in front of us but the waiter assured us it was very good. We tucked in and spread the tomatoes, oil and herbs on to the bread with a knife. Absolutely divine and stupidly simple. These are just wonderful with grilled meats, mozzarella, stirred into hot pasta or used to top a salad. Only use ripe flavourful tomatoes in late summer when they are at their sweetest. The recipe will work with any size of tomato but round ones will take longer than cherry or baby plum. See photo on previous page.

**METHOD**

Heat the oven to 180°C (350°F/Gas 6). Cut the tomatoes in half (around the equator, not pole to pole) and put them on a baking tray. Season with salt and pepper. Bake in the oven for 10–20 minutes, depending on the size, until they start to soften and shrivel. Remove the tray from the oven and scatter over the oregano and drizzle over the olive oil. Return to the oven for 10–15 minutes or until they just start to collapse and brown. Remove from the oven and allow to cool a little before serving with crusty bread.

400 g (14 oz) ripe flavourful tomatoes (cherry, small plum or round)

Salt and freshly ground black pepper

1 teaspoon finely chopped oregano

3 tablespoons extra-virgin olive oil

INSALATA DI OVOLI, SEDANO E PARMIGIANO REGGIANO

# Mushroom, Celery and Parmesan Salad

**SERVES 4** (as a starter)

In autumn, Romans go mad for the egg-shaped *ovoli* mushrooms. Pushing up through the forest floor, they look like boiled eggs which then unfurl themselves into orange heads hiding creamy fragile gills. These are so delicate in flavour that they are often served raw in a salad. Maria, from the restaurant Al Ceppo in Rome, told me that she adds pine nuts to her mushroom salad so that you have something to chew. She says it slows you down when eating the dish and helps to release the flavour of the *ovoli*. As these are almost impossible to buy outside Italy I have substituted them for an assortment of oyster, chestnut and shiitake. This salad is best if made a couple of hours before eating; you would think the mushrooms would become soft but actually the dressing enhances the flavour. However, the rocket (arugula) will wilt, so leave it until just before serving to add it. This is ideal for entertaining as a light starter assuming, of course, your guests like mushrooms!

## METHOD

Toast the pine nuts in a dry frying pan over a medium heat, shaking the pan frequently, until golden. Set aside on a plate to cool. Prepare the mushrooms (only wash them if they are very dirty) and put them into a bowl with the rocket, celery and pine nuts. Whisk the lemon juice, oil and salt together in a separate bowl and pour over the salad. Toss gently so that the mushrooms become coated in the dressing. Tip into a serving dish and scatter over the Parmesan shavings.

50 g (2 oz) pine nuts

350 g (12 oz) assorted mushrooms, brushed clean and cut into 3 mm (1/4 in) thick slices

50 g (2 oz) rocket (arugula)

1 celery stick, finely sliced

juice of 1/2 lemon

4 tablespoons extra-virgin olive oil

1/2 teaspoon salt

25 g (1 oz) shaved Parmesan or Emmental

FRITTATA ROMANA

# *Frittata Stuffed with Ricotta and Parmesan*

**MAKES 2 FRITTATE** (Serves 4 as antipasti)

We love this dish for an impressive breakfast or a quick lunch. We serve it with a few cut and seasoned tomatoes on the side, and a little parsley or basil. Soft herbs or leftovers such as the Grilled Courgette Salad (see page 40), Wilted Tomatoes (see page 45), cooked peas or spinach are perfect stirred into the ricotta, which, as the frittata sets, turns into a light foaming centre.

**METHOD**

Heat the oven to 180°C (350°F/Gas 6). Start by making the frittata base. In an omelette or non-stick frying pan with a base diameter of 15–20 cm (6–8 in), melt half of the butter over a medium heat until it foams. Beat 2 of the eggs in a bowl with 1 tablespoon of the Parmesan, and season. Pour this into the pan and cook until it just sets; there should be only a little wet egg mixture on the surface.

While the frittata base is cooking, combine all the ingredients for the filling in a bowl. Spread half of the filling over the centre of the frittata. Using a spatula, flip one half of the frittata over the other half, making a half moon, to seal the filling inside. Transfer to an ovenproof plate and into the oven. Cook until the egg is set; around 5 minutes should do it. Meanwhile, make the next frittata in the same way with the remaining ingredients. To serve, slide off the plates (careful, the plates will be hot!) and slice. If you want this for a more substantial meal, serve with fresh or Wilted Tomatoes (see page 45) and Warm Farro Salad (see page 33) or crusty bread.

**FOR THE FRITTATA**

25 g (1 oz) salted butter

4 eggs

2 heaped tablespoons finely grated Parmesan

Salt and freshly ground black pepper

**FOR THE FILLING**

100 g ($3^1/_2$ oz) ricotta

2 heaped tablespoons finely grated Parmesan

3 heaped tablespoons cooked sliced vegetables, or 1 tablespoon finely chopped soft herbs

Salt and freshly ground black pepper

FRITTATA DI MENTA AL SUGO FINTO

# Mint Frittata in Tomato Sauce

**SERVES 2** (as a snack or light lunch)

This dish is also called *Uova* in Trippa alla Romana as the strips of frittata in tomato sauce resembles the Romans' beloved dish of tripe in tomato sauce. It can be bought as a takeaway snack from *Supplizio* in Rome and makes a great breakfast or light lunch.

## METHOD

Heat the tomato sauce in a saucepan over a medium heat. Meanwhile, beat together the eggs, mint, Parmesan and seasoning in a bowl. Make the frittata following the same method as the Spinach and Cheese Frittata on page 70. When cooked, turn on to a plate and cut the frittata into fat chips around 2 cm (¾ in) wide by 6 cm (2½ in) long. Put these into the tomato sauce and stir gently. Serve in warm bowls garnished with the Parmesan and a little more mint, alongside some crusty bread.

500 ml (17 fl oz) *Sugo Finto* tomato sauce (page 137)

4 eggs

2 tablespoons finely chopped fresh mint, plus extra to serve

15 g (¹/₂ oz) finely grated Parmesan, plus extra to serve

Salt and freshly ground black pepper

CAVOLO ROSSO STUFATO CON GUANCIALE

# Slow-cooked Red Cabbage with Bacon

**SERVES 6** (as a side)

Claudia Paiella from her wonderful Roman restaurant Enoteca Corsi gave us this almost black dish to try as one of their specialities and we were won over. It is made with *guanciale,* cured pork cheeks, and is a very good juicy carrier to have with drier meats such as the *Abbacchio* on page 177, *Porchetta* on page 167 or simple sausages.

### METHOD

Cut the cabbage into thin slices and then chop them into 5 cm (2 in) long pieces so that you have manageable pieces to eat with a fork. Fry the *guanciale,* onion and salt in the oil in a large high-sided frying pan over a medium heat for about 5–10 minutes. When the onion is soft, add the cabbage and raisins and let it cook for around 5 minutes more. Add the wine and let it evaporate. Pour in the stock or water, turn the heat to low and continue to cook for 40 minutes to 1 hour, uncovered, or until the cabbage is really soft and wilted. The majority of the liquid should have evaporated and the mixture should be moist but not liquid. Serve warm.

1 medium red cabbage (approx. 800 g/1 lb 12 oz)

150 g (5 oz) *guanciale* or streaky unsmoked bacon, cut into 1 cm (1/2 in) wide strips

1 medium onion (approx. 100g/ 3 1/2 oz), finely chopped

1/2 teaspoon fine salt

4 tablespoons extra-virgin olive oil

100 g (3 1/2 oz) raisins

150 ml (5 fl oz) red wine

800 ml–1 litre (27–34 fl oz) homemade vegetable stock (see page 107) or water

FORMAGGIO DI CAPRA FRITTO CON SORBETTO DI PEPERONI ROSSI

# *Deep-fried Goats' Cheese with Red Pepper Sorbet*

## *FOR THE DEEP FRIED GOATS' CHEESE*

SERVES 6

At the wonderful Al Ceppo restaurant, we were inspired by a triumphant looking dish of hot deep-fried mozzarella-filled courgette (zucchini) flowers stood upright on a plate and encircled with small domes of cold red (bell) pepper sorbet resembling cherry tomatoes (see photo on previous page). We loved the combination of flavours as well as contrasting temperatures. As courgette flowers are difficult to find, our version is made with hot goats' cheese, which melts inside a deep-fried breadcrumb crust. It's wonderful with the cold spicy sorbet. Depending on the width of the log of cheese, you will need to cut it into six or twelve slices. As an alternative to deep frying the goats' cheese, it can be grilled. To do this place the cheese slices on a piece of sourdough bread and scatter over a little thyme and black pepper. Grill it until golden and serve straight away with the sorbet.

METHOD

Heat the oil in a large high-sided frying pan or deep-fat fryer to around 175°C (345°F) or hot enough to make a small piece of bread sizzle when it hits the fat. If you are using a pan, ensure the oil comes no further than halfway up the sides, but is deep enough to completely cover the coated cheese slices. Put the flour, egg(s) and breadcrumbs into 3 separate bowls. Slice the goats' cheese log, depending on the width, into 6 large slices or 12 small slices around 1.5 cm (½ in) thick. If it crumbles while you cut it, warm the blade of the knife in hot water. Dip each slice into the flour, then the egg and finally the breadcrumbs. Gently lower the coated pieces into the hot oil and fry for around 1–2 minutes or until golden brown. If they start to split take them out quickly. Remove from the oil with a slotted spoon and drain on kitchen paper.

Groundnut or sunflower oil, for frying

25 g (1 oz/scant ¼ cup) '00' or plain (all-purpose) flour

1–2 eggs, beaten

50 g (2 oz) breadcrumbs

400 g (14 oz) goats' cheese log

DEEP-FRIED GOATS' CHEESE,
PAGE 56

MOZZARELLA ON
SOURDOUGH CROSTINI
AND ANCHOVY BUTTER,
PAGE 78

RED PEPPER SORBET,
PAGE 56

## *FOR THE RED PEPPER SORBET*

**SERVES 10–12** (as a starter or side)

We have a tub of this spicy savoury sorbet permanently in our freezer as it is so versatile. You can dress it up to look like cherry tomatoes, serve it with hot cheese on toast, melt it over risotto, use it as a chilled dip for Parmesan crisps, a garnish for chilled soups or have it with anything hot and fried such as the Deep-Fried Goats' Cheese (see opposite).

**METHOD**

Heat the oven to 200°C (400°F/Gas 7). Put the whole peppers on a baking tray and bake for around 45 minutes or until the skins are black and blistered. Remove the peppers from the oven, tip them into a large bowl and cover it with baking parchment. Allow the peppers to sweat and cool down. Once cool, peel away their skins and also discard their seeds and cores, so you are left with just the soft flesh.

Put the peppers into a food processor with the remaining ingredients and blend until smooth. Taste and adjust the salt and heat levels, adding extra Tabasco or chilli as necessary; it should be punchy and sweet in flavour. When cold, churn in an ice-cream machine or follow the method of making sorbet by hand on page 240.

6 large red (bell) peppers

100 ml (3$^1$/$_2$ fl oz) water

2 tablespoons liquid glucose

Juice of 1 lemon

3 tablespoons caster (superfine) sugar

$^1$/$_2$–1 teaspoon fine salt

Few drops of Tabasco (hot-pepper) sauce or $^1$/$_4$ teaspoon chilli powder, to taste

# Picnic at Villa Borghese

Street food is widely available in Rome, whether it is a slice of pizza (see page 84), the little stuffed rice balls *Supplì* (see page 97), filled *panini* or a hunk of *pizza Romana*, the squashy focaccia particular to Rome (see page 60),or the bread made in the hills called *genzano* to eat with salami or pecorino cheese.

Grab a selection and head to one of the tranquil parks to enjoy the shade and park life. We love the gardens of Villa Borghese as it is so central and full of statues, avenues, tall trees and home to bicycle buggies and segways – fun when you are being a tourist!

PIZZA BIANCA ROMANA

# Roman Focaccia Bread

MAKES 1 LOAF

It was two o'clock one sunny Sunday lunchtime and the noise of cutlery, chattering families and clinking glasses echoed around the surrounding flats in a neighbourhood near San Lorenzo, east of central Rome. We were with our friends Stefania and Piero having a lazy lunch. A basket of *pizza bianca* was in the centre of the table and next to it was a plate of ripe green figs and another plate of just-sliced translucent Parma ham. Stefania told me to slice open a piece of the bread and stuff it with quarters of fig and slices of ham. Closing it up like a sandwich, I bit into this gloriously satisfying mouthful of chewy bread, sweet figs and salty ham.

This is not actually pizza but more of a focaccia-style bread that splits open and used for *panini* or thick sandwiches. We loved it on the shoot for our picnic photographs stuffed with green tomatoes and mozzarella. The dough needs to prove overnight, so make the dough the day before you want to bake it. Alessandro Roscioli, whose family have been baking for years, gave us his recipe below. His bakery Antico Forno Roscioli and his restaurant Salumeria Roscioli are two of our favourite haunts. Even though we have said to use strong flour, different brands have varying absorbency so be prepared to add more water or flour in some cases.

METHOD

This will make a very wet dough so it is best done in a stand mixer. Mix all the ingredients except the oil together with a dough hook at a slow speed for 5 minutes, then turn the speed to high and continue to mix for 10 minutes. If you don't have a stand mixer, use a dough scraper to knead the dough in the bowl. Remove the bowl from the mixer, cover it with baking parchment and leave in the fridge for 20–22 hours.

Remove the bowl from the fridge and let it warm up for a couple of hours in a warm room. Right, now you are going to knead a very wet dough. Be firm, show it who's boss and use plenty of oil. Firstly wipe an oven tray, your work surface, spatula and hands with a layer of oil. Tip the dough from the bowl on to the oiled surface.

Using your fingertips, press the dough into a rough flat rectangle around 25 x 20 cm (10 x 8 in). Lift and fold one of the short edges of the dough into the centre, then fold over the opposite one. Press your fingertips into it to push it out to the same rectangle as before and fold the short edges in again. Do this twice more. This will help to create air bubbles inside. Put the dough on to the oiled baking tray and let it relax for 10 minutes. Push it out with your fingertips to around 30 x 25 cm (12 x 10 in) leaving imprints in the surface. It is easier to do this in 2 or 3 stages, each time letting the dough relax for 10 minutes between pressings. Drizzle oil over the top of the dough and gently wipe it over with your fingers making sure it is all covered. Leave in a warm place to rise for 1 hour or until doubled in size and it looks puffy and bubbly.

Heat the oven to 220°C (430°F/ Gas 9) using the top and bottom heat and turn the fan off if you can. Gently push your fingertips into the surface of the *pizza bianca* dough one last time and carefully pull the short edges outwards. Evenly scatter over some salt. Bake in the oven for 15–20 minutes or until rich golden brown. Remove from the oven and cool to room temperature on a wire rack before serving.

500 g (1 lb 2 oz/ 4 cups) strong white bread flour

325 ml (11 fl oz) water

75 ml (2$^1$/$_2$ fl oz) whole milk

10 g ($^1$/$_2$ oz) coarse organic salt, plus extra to finish

7 g ($^1$/$_4$ oz) sugar

3 g ($^1$/$_8$ oz) beer yeast or active dried yeast

Extra-virgin olive oil

LAGANA

# Seeded Wine Crackers

SERVES 8 (makes about 30 crackers)

This is a dish from ancient Roman times and would have been enjoyed during the reign of Julius Caesar. Apparently he was not keen on drinking alcohol as he liked to talk and glean information from his guests. *Lagana* were simply pieces of fried pastry frequently used in place of a spoon for scooping up dips or vegetable purées. In this version, red wine and pepper is used. Mark Grant, who translated the recipe from the Latin, suggests you should crush the pepper by hand 'so as to provide little explosions of fire when the biscuit is being eaten'. Originally the crackers would have been fried, but we like to bake them to a crisp in the oven. We've also experimented with adding seeds and herbs; if you do use them mix them at the start or roll them into the dough with a rolling pin to secure them. *Lagana* are also thought to be the forerunner of lasagne. For a gluten-free version use buckwheat flour. See photo overleaf.

## METHOD

Heat the oven to 200°C (400°F/Gas 7) and line a baking tray with baking parchment. Combine all the ingredients in a mixing bowl and knead until you have a smooth dough. Flour the work surface well and roll out the dough to around 1 mm thick. Cut into rectangles – mine are usually around 8 x 5 cm (3 x 2 in) – with a knife or a wiggly-edged pasta wheel. Transfer them to the lined tray and cook for around 10 minutes until lightly browned and crisp. Remove from the trays and allow to cool before storing them in an airtight container for up to 10 days. Serve with ricotta, the Hot Fish Pickle (see opposite) and Walnut and Feta Pesto (see page 67).

175 g (6 oz) wholemeal (whole-wheat), spelt or buckwheat flour

1 tablespoon olive oil

60 ml (2 fl oz) red wine

40 ml (1 fl oz) goat or cow's milk

1 teaspoon crushed black peppercorns

1/2 teaspoon salt

Sunflower or groundnut oil for frying (optional)

OPTIONAL FLAVOURINGS

1 tablespoon sesame seeds,

1 tablespoon black onion seeds,

1 teaspoon finely chopped rosemary leaves or thyme leaves

SALSA DI PESCE PICCANTE

# *Hot Fish Pickle*

SERVES 4–6

This peppery little concoction comes from Europe's oldest surviving recipe book *Of Culinary Matters*, which is thought by many to have been written by Apicius, the ancient Roman cook and gourmet, around the time of Julius Caesar. Who knows, it may well have been Julius's favourite nibble with a glass of wine. Pickled fish, known as *garum* or *liquamen*, was left to ferment and mature and then bottled to use as a seasoning, but this version is used fresh and as a dip. We know that the ancient Romans liked to eat *panem et pulmentum*: bread and relish. These types of relish were eaten with *Lagana*, a crisp thin bread that was fried and flavoured with wine (see opposite). We like to eat them with creamy ricotta as it binds the relish to the crackers. We have kept the ingredients here pretty much the same as described in John Edwards' book *The Roman Cookery of Apicius*. The 'hot' in the name of this refers to the use of black pepper as chilli wasn't around then, but if you like things spicy, do add a little fresh or dried red chilli to taste. See photo overleaf.

METHOD

Combine the wet ingredients together with the pepper and garlic in a large bowl. Next stir in the herbs, celery and sardines together with a spoon in a bowl, gently breaking up the fish as you stir. (This can be stored in the fridge for 1 day if you don't want to use it immediately.)

Stir through the salt just before serving, or the leaves will wilt prematurely. The pickle is still good up to 3 days later, if it doesn't all get eaten straight away, but the vibrancy of the bright celery leaves and parsley will fade. Serve at room temperature with Lagana, Seeded Wine Crackers, on opposite page, and ricotta, or on toasted sourdough bread.

2 tablespoons white wine

2 tablespoons vinegar

1 teaspoon Dijon mustard

2 teaspoons mild, runny honey

4 tablespoons extra-virgin olive oil

$1/4$ teaspoon freshly ground black pepper

1 small garlic clove, finely chopped

15 g ($1/2$) flat-leaf parsley, finely chopped

3 tablespoons finely chopped basil leaves

2 tablespoons finely chopped mint leaves

1 celery heart (the pale and tender inner part) and the leaves, roughly chopped

160 g (5$1/2$ oz) tinned sardines, tuna or mackerel, drained weight

Salt to taste

SEEDED WINE
CRACKERS,
PAGE 62

OLIVE, FENNEL
& MINT SALSA,
PAGE 66

WALNUT & FETA PESTO,
PAGE 67

RICOTTA

HOT FISH PICKLE,
PAGE 63

SALSA DI OLIVE

# Olive, Fennel and Mint Salsa

SERVES 4–6

Did you hear the one about the dyslexic who went to the toga party as a goat? (Living with two dyslexics we have all developed a sense of humour about the subject!) Inspired by an ancient Roman recipe, this is one of our favourite salsas to make if we have guests wearing togas – or dressed as goats for that matter. Our friend and Latin teacher, Anne Hudson, had the idea of adding fresh fennel and soaking the fennel seeds to soften them; it makes the salsa even better. It is lovely to dip into with crackers, serve on simply cooked fish, such as the Fish and Bronze Fennel in a Parcel on page 151, or tossed into hot pasta or spelt for a vegan dish. Do use the best olives you can find and preferably pit them yourself: they will have a lot more flavour. If you have to use ready pitted olives, reduce the quantity to 75 g (2$^1$/$_2$ oz) each of green and black olives. See photo on previous page.

## METHOD

Pit the olives by squashing them with the flat of a large cook's knife to help the stone pop out. Chop the flesh into small cubes around 5 mm (1/4 in) in size. Combine all the ingredients in a bowl and season with salt and pepper to taste. Serve at room temperature. This will keep in the fridge for up to 3 days.

100 g (3$^1$/$_2$ oz) unpitted green olives

100 g (3$^1$/$_2$ oz) unpitted black olives

1$^1$/$_2$ teaspoons ground cumin

1 teaspoon fennel seeds, soaked in warm water for 10 minutes

Handful of coriander (cilantro) leaves, roughly chopped

Handful of flat-leaf parsley, roughly chopped

1 fennel bulb, woody parts removed, chopped into 1 cm (1/2 in) cubes

1 tablespoon roughly chopped mint leaves

1 teaspoon finely chopped rosemary leaves

3 tablespoons extra-virgin olive oil

2 tablespoons red wine vinegar

Salt and freshly ground black pepper

PESTO DI FETA E NOCI

# Walnut and Feta Pesto

SERVES 6–8

This is based on the herb pastes of ancient Rome; they were probably the forerunner of pesto, says Mark Grant in his book *Roman Cookery*. Eat this with the Seeded Wine Crackers on page 62, bread or dollop on to boiled eggs or potatoes. Various herbs or leaves, such as lettuce, watercress or spinach, can be used. Feta is the closest we now have to Roman soft cheese. These are good made with hazelnuts, almonds or pine nuts if you want to try different combinations. See photo on previous page.

## METHOD

Heat the oven to 200°C (400°F/ Gas 7). Toast the nuts for around 10 minutes until they start to brown to bring out their flavour. Remove from the oven and allow to cool. Put all the ingredients into a food processor and whizz together until you get a rough pesto. Taste and adjust seasoning as necessary. This will store for up to 3 days in the fridge.

75 g (2$^1$/$_2$ oz) walnuts

50 g (2 oz) feta

1 baby gem lettuce

large handful mint leaves (approx. 10 g/$^1$/$_2$ oz)

15 g ($^1$/$_2$ oz) flat-leaf parsley leaves (no coarse stalks)

2 tablespoons white or red wine vinegar

5 tablespoons extra-virgin olive oil

Good twist black pepper

$^1$/$_4$ teaspoon salt

GLOBI

# Cheese and Honey Pastries

**SERVES 8–10** (makes about 40 pastries)

*Globi*, pronounced to rhyme with 'blobby', means 'globes' in Latin. But despite the rather silly sounding name, these sweet and salty morsels are just lovely as a pre-dinner nibble with wine or fizz. They were written about by Cato the Elder, an ancient Roman censor who disapproved of decadent living – so maybe he wouldn't have approved of the fizz!

## METHOD

Grate the cheese and rub it into the flour in a bowl with your fingertips. When the mixture resembles breadcrumbs, add the beaten egg and continue to use your hands to work it into a dough. Break off small pieces and roll them into balls the size of a large marble between your palms.

Fill one third of a large, high-sided pan with oil and heat until a small cube of bread sizzles immediately when dropped into the oil. Alternatively, use a deep-fat fryer if you have one. Fry the pastry balls in batches for around 3–5 minutes or until golden brown. Turn the heat down a little if the oil starts to foam. Remove with a slotted spoon and drain on kitchen paper.

Heat the honey in a frying pan over a medium heat and toss the balls in it to coat them all over. Put the seeds on to a plate and roll the sticky pastries in them. Serve at room temperature.

200 g (7 oz) Cheddar or firm goats' cheese

100 g (3¹/₂ oz) spelt flour

1 egg, beaten

Sunflower or groundnut oil, for frying

60 ml (2 fl oz) mild honey

2 tablespoons poppy or sesame seeds

FRITTATA DI SPINACI E FORMAGGIO DI PECORA FRESCA

# Spinach and Cheese Frittata

**SERVES 6** (as antipasti)

Because the Jewish people have always travelled, whether through their own volition or not, they have had a massive impact on the culinary world as with them they brought recipes and methods of cooking from previous homes.

This is one of cookery writer Claudia Roden's recipes, which she believes comes from the Italian Jews who left Italy for Ottoman lands. I love the combination of spinach and feta, and frequently make this for breakfast for the family, using up leftover cooked potatoes. Also, if you have any Silvia's Sautéed Spinach with Pine Nuts and Raisins (see page 27) left over, do use it for this. In fact, it is lovely to have the crunch of pine nuts and the sweetness of raisins in this frittata, so I often add a couple of tablespoons of each anyway.

### METHOD

Remove and discard any tough stems from the spinach. Wash the spinach in a colander and tip it into a large lidded saucepan on a low heat. Put the lid on and steam the spinach in the residual water for about 2–3 minutes until it has wilted down. Drain away the liquid and, when it is cool enough to touch, squeeze out the remaining excess water. Cut the spinach coarsely.

Heat the grill to a medium heat. In a large bowl, lightly beat the eggs. Add the potato, spinach, feta, nutmeg and seasoning, and stir gently. In an ovenproof non stick frying pan around 24 cm (9¹/₂ in) wide, heat the oil. Pour in the egg mixture and cook over a low heat for about 10–15 minutes, until the bottom has set. Transfer the pan to under the grill and cook for about 5 minutes until firm and lightly browned. Turn out on to a plate and serve hot or cold, cut in wedges.

400 g (14 oz) spinach leaves

5 eggs

1 medium potato, boiled and peeled (see page 29 for method), and chopped

200 g (7 oz) feta, crumbled

1/4 teaspoon ground nutmeg

Salt and freshly ground black pepper

2 tablespoons extra-virgin olive oil

INSALATA DI BORLOTTI

# Wendy's Borlotti Bean Salad

SERVES 4–6 (as a side)

GUEST RECIPE
Wendy Holloway
GUEST RECIPE

Our friend Wendy Holloway has lived in Rome for more than 30 years, and she runs guided food tours of the city and cookery courses at her house. This is one of her favourite recipes that she showed us, using fresh borlotti beans we picked up at the market. She thinks these beans are so pretty, like someone has hand painted them; each one is different. Dried beans can be used instead, they just aren't so pretty, but the flavour is the same. If you are in a real hurry, use tinned beans, which I have often done as this is a great standby salad. This dressing is also wonderful poured over blackened peeled peppers or hot potatoes. Try it with the *Porchetta* on page 167.

## METHOD

If you are using dried beans, soak them overnight in a bowl of clean water. Drain and cook them in a large pan of salted water with the bay leaves and garlic for around 1 hour or until soft.(If the skins refuse to soften add a level teaspoon of bicarbonate of soda to the water.) For fresh beans, cook them the same way for roughly 30 minutes, until they are soft and creamy. Tinned beans need just to be drained and reheated in fresh water in a saucepan with the bay leaves and garlic for a few minutes.

While the beans are cooking, finely chop the red onion. Put the rosemary leaves (discard the stalks) and sage on top of the chopped onion and finely chop the herbs into the onion until everything amalgamates. Put this mixture into a large bowl with the oil and balsamic. Drain the beans, retaining a little cooking water, and immediately toss them into the balsamic mixture in the bowl. Leave to cool and they will soak up the wonderful flavour. If the beans dry out, splash in some of the reserved cooking liquid. Serve at room temperature.

250 g (9 oz) dried or uncooked fresh borlotti beans, or 500 g (1 lb 2 oz) tinned borlotti beans

2 bay leaves

1 garlic clove, lightly crushed

1 small red onion

10 cm (4 in) sprig rosemary

Few sage leaves

5 tablespoons extra-virgin olive oil

1 tablespoon balsamic vinegar

Salt

PEPERONATA ALLA ROMANA

# *Roast Red and Yellow Pepper Relish*

SERVES 4-6

Generally in a *peperonata*, the peppers are cooked in a pan, but a little forethought transforms this everyday side dish into something rather special. This recipe is from Enoteca Corsi, a wonderful bustling Roman trattoria. However, my twist is to use oven-roasted rather than pan-fried peppers; I blacken them in the oven and then peel away their blistered skins to reveal the intense sweetness of the flesh underneath. This dish keeps well in the fridge for a few days, so make a large batch – it goes quickly. Eat it with roast chicken, baked fish, Wendy's Borlotti Bean Salad (see opposite) or simply bread and cheese.

4 red or yellow peppers, or mix of both

100 g ($3^{1}/_{2}$ oz) potatoes

4 tablespoons extra-virgin olive oil

1 garlic clove, peeled and halved

1 shallot or small onion, finely chopped

1 tinned anchovy fillet in oil

1 tablespoon capers, rinsed well

100 g ($3^{1}/_{2}$ oz) black olives

$^{1}/_{2}$ teaspoon fine salt

50 ml (2 fl oz) white wine

1 tablespoon flat-leaf parsley to garnish (optional)

## METHOD

Heat the oven to 200°C (400°F/Gas 7). Cook the whole peppers on a tray until blackened, blistered and soft. It will take around 30–45 minutes. Remove from the oven and put them into a bowl using tongs. Cover the bowl with a plate and leave to cool and sweat for 30 minutes. Peel the peppers under cold water and discard the cores and seeds. Tear them into long strips around 3 cm (1 in) wide and set aside.

Boil the potatoes whole and in their skins until cooked through. Depending on their size, this can take up to 1 hour; a skewer should slide easily into the potatoes when they are done. Drain and peel while hot. You can do this easily with a cloth to hold the potato and a dinner knife to scrape away the skin. Chop into 1 cm (½ in) cubes. Heat the oil in a large lidded frying pan and fry the potatoes, garlic and onion over a medium heat until the onions are soft and translucent. Add the anchovy and stir through until melted and dissolved into the onions. Add the capers, olives, peppers and salt and toss together. Pour in the wine and allow to evaporate for a few minutes. Cover the pan and continue to cook over a moderate heat for 5 minutes. Taste and adjust the seasoning as necessary. Decorate the dish with parsley if you like it. Serve warm or allow to come to room temperature.

BRUSCHETTA ALLA ROMANA

# Roman Bruschetta

SERVES 6

*Bruschetta*, pronounced 'brusketta', is served all over Italy, but it seems even more so in Rome. Our children love it and even eat it at breakfast before school. With properly ripe tomatoes, fresh herbs and really good single estate extra-virgin olive oil it is a winner of a dish at any time. We like to use a strong, green, peppery olive oil for this, such as a robust Tuscan. Our favourite Roman version is served at Roman restaurant Pierluigi, where cherry tomatoes are mixed with herbs, chilli and garlic. For the best flavour toast your bread on a hot barbecue grill, but failing that use the oven grill or a toaster. This tomato topping is also wonderful stirred into hot pasta with cubes of mozzarella, or served with fish or grilled chicken. The toast can be made in advance but it shouldn't be topped until just before serving.

ROMAN BRUSCHETTA,
PAGE 76

## METHOD

Rub the garlic clove over one side of each of the toasted breads. Gently mix the remaining ingredients together in a large bowl and season to taste. If necessary, add more thyme, chilli or salt to achieve a full-flavoured result. Top the garlic toasts with the tomato mixture and serve straight away.

6 slices thickly sliced sourdough bread, toasted both sides

1 small garlic clove, peeled

200 g (7 oz) sweet ripe tomatoes, cut into bite-size pieces

2 tablespoons best quality extra-virgin olive oil

12 large basil leaves, roughly chopped

1 heaped teaspoon thyme leaves

2 heaped tablespoons roughly chopped flat-leaf parsley

$1/2$–1 red chilli, roughly chopped, to taste

Salt and freshly ground black pepper

BONE MARROW,
PARMESAN & PARSLEY
TOAST, PAGE 77

MOZARRELLA ON
SOURDOUGH WITH ANCHOVY
BUTTER, PAGE 78

CROSTINI COL MEROLLO

# Bone Marrow, Parmesan and Parsley Toasts

SERVES 6

This meaty treat reminds me of the fried bread of my childhood made from beef dripping. If I hadn't read this recipe in Ada Boni's book *Italian Regional Cooking* I probably wouldn't have tried it, but now I am converted. People can be squeamish about eating marrow but if you don't tell them what it is and get them to try it, they love it. Our friend Nick Sandler mixes it with Parmesan and parsley, which is even better.

**METHOD**

Heat the oven to 200°C (400°F/ Gas 7). Scrape out the fatty marrow from the bone and mix together in a bowl with the cheese, parsley, and seasoning. Spread a heaped tablespoon on to each slice of sourdough bread. Put them into the oven on a rack until the topping melts and the breads become toast.

1 beef
marrowbone
(approx. 160 g/
5 1/2 oz), halved
lengthways
(you can ask your
butcher to do this)

25 g (1 oz)
Parmesan,
finely grated

Handful of
flat-leaf parsley,
tough stems
removed and
finely chopped

Salt and freshly
ground black
pepper to taste

6 slices thickly
sliced sourdough
bread

CROSTINI CON MOZZARELLA E BURRO ALLE ALICI

# Mozzarella on Sourdough Crostini with Anchovy Butter

SERVES 6

Melting mozzarella on crisp sourdough toast splashed in an anchovy butter is so moreish you will find yourself licking the pan! We make them when we have people round for drinks and they are wolfed down. Prepare the bread and butter, slice and drain the cheese, and pop them under the grill as the doorbell rings. See photo on previous page.

METHOD

Cut the mozzarella into 6 slices and put them into a sieve to drain while you make up the sauce. Melt the butter in a small saucepan with the anchovies, stirring with a wooden spoon to break them up. Set aside. Take the mozzarella out of the sieve and lay on to each of the bread slices. Put the crostini under a hot grill to melt the cheese and let the crusts brown. Gently heat the anchovy butter until it's runny again, put the crostini on to a serving dish and drizzle over the butter. Serve straight away.

1 x 125 g (4 oz) *mozzarella di buffala* (buffalo mozzarella) ball

20 g (3/4 oz) salted butter

2 tinned anchovy fillets in oil

6 thick slices sourdough bread (around 2 cm/ 3/4 in thick)

BURRO E ALICI

# Anchovy and Butter Toasts

Ah the simple pleasures of life! We were first given this dish on the outskirts of Rome when enjoying a tasting of Prosecco. The wine maker assured us it would be a wonderful combination as the bubbly dryness of a good Prosecco cuts the creamy butterfat and oily fish. He was right; another Roman combination of three things – butter, toast and anchovy – that we almost always have in our cupboard should we wish to rustle up a quick treat. See photo opposite.

METHOD

Toast sourdough bread in a toaster, on a grill or, better still, over a charcoal fire. Allow the bread to cool a little then top with the best organic unsalted butter you can find and lay over a little salty anchovy. Pour a chilled flute of Prosecco and forget all your woes.

# Street Food

From the *thermopolia*, a 'hot shop' where quick meals were eaten in or taken away by the 'plebs' of ancient Rome, to the numerous delis and bakeries of today, Romans have always had a penchant for street food. As kitchens have either been non-existent or uncomfortably small in Roman homes, food was often bought and eaten on the street, a way of life that has continued since emperors ruled the city.

*Cibo da strada*, or street food, is easily found and bought for a few euro. Make sure you try *Supplì*, the long deep-fried rice balls filled with mozzarella (see page 97), crispy Roman pizza by the slice (see page 84), panini filled with cheese or cured meats, *Porchetta* roast pork (see page 167) in a bun and fried meatballs made of slowly cooked beef (see page 90), all of which are easily found on streets. There is also a recent addition to street food, in the form of *trapizzino* – an invention by chef Stefano Callegari – which is a triangular sandwich filled with a Roman classic stew.

Morsels of fried food have been served in Rome for thousands of years, but it was the Jewish immigrants who brought the tradition of using a batter. An idea they took from the Arabs in Sicily. The fryers, or *friggitori*, would coat artichokes, ricotta, lamb chops, brains, courgettes (zucchinis) and their flowers in batter and fry them in vats of bubbling olive oil. Vegetables such as artichokes were easy to find and cheap, and by frying them even the outside leaves, which are usually discarded, could be eaten and, more importantly, sold.

IL GRAN FRITTO MISTO

# A Big Mixed Fry-Up

SERVES 6–8

## FOR 'DRY' INGREDIENTS

SUCH AS FISH, ARTICHOKES, CAULIFLOWER,
MUSHROOMS, SWEETBREADS OR BRAIN

'*Il gran fritto misto*', literally 'a big mixed fry-up', sounds like it should be served held high on a huge silver platter by a waistcoated Italian waiter. We cook our *fritto misto* in two ways: in a batter to coat dry foods such as cauliflower and mushrooms so that the food steams within, and in a flour coating for wet foods such as courgettes (zucchinis) and calamari; if you use a batter for foods with a wet surface, it will just slide off and not coat them properly. And just to bring this traditional dish up to date, we have supplied a gluten-free batter, which works very well for those who can't have wheat flour.

METHOD

Heat the oil in a large high-sided frying pan or deep-fat fryer to around 175°C (345°F) or hot enough to make a small piece of bread sizzle when it hits the fat. If you are using a pan, ensure the oil comes no further than halfway up the sides, but is deep enough to completely cover the pieces to be fried. Make up your chosen batter by whisking the flour and egg together in a large bowl. Add the milk little by little and keep whisking to get rid of any lumps. You need a runny smooth consistency like that of double (heavy) cream. Cut the fish, vegetables or offal (see below for how to prepare brain) into small even-sized pieces that can be picked up with your fingers and eaten in a couple of bites; a floret of cauliflower or a short stick of courgette (zucchini) for example. Dip each piece into the batter and allow the excess to drip off for a few seconds. Gently lower into the hot fat and fry until golden brown. Most morsels of food dipped in batter take around 3 minutes to cook.

*This is enough to coat 500 g (1 lb 2 oz) of a mixture or one of the opposite.*

Groundnut or sunflower oil, for frying

**FLOUR BATTER**

125 g (4 oz/1 cup) '00' or plain (all-purpose) flour

1 egg

125 ml (4 fl oz) milk

**GLUTEN-FREE BATTER**

100 g (3 1/2 oz/ generous 3/4 cup) cornflour (corn starch)

1 egg

40 ml (1 1/2 fl oz) milk

# TO PREPARE THE BRAIN

**METHOD**

Clean the brain under cold running water to remove any blood. Detach and discard the membrane covering it. Cut it into quarters. In a large pan, bring the water to a gentle boil, add the vinegar and then poach the brain for 5 minutes. Remove from the water with a slotted spoon and let it cool to room temperature. Chill in the fridge for 30 minutes. Remove from the fridge and then follow the instructions for coating and frying opposite.

500 g (1 lb 2 oz) calf brain

1 litre (34 fl oz) water

2 tablespoons white wine vinegar

# FOR 'WET' INGREDIENTS

**SUCH AS COURGETTES (ZUCCHINIS), RED (BELL) PEPPERS AND CALAMARI**

**METHOD**

Cut the vegetables into bite-size batons and the calamari into rings around 1 cm (1/2 in) wide. Heat the oil in a large high-sided frying pan or deep-fat fryer to around 175°C (345°F) or hot enough to make a small piece of bread sizzle when it hits the fat. If you are using a pan, ensure the oil comes no further than halfway up the sides, but is deep enough to completely cover the pieces to be fried. Sift the flour into a large bowl and line another large dish with kitchen paper. Pour the milk into a separate bowl and put the pieces of food, a few at a time, into the milk to soak for 1–2 minutes. Lift them out with a slotted spoon, giving it a couple of taps to drain most of the liquid. Put them into the flour and toss them with your hands. Gently lower the pieces into the hot oil and cook for around 2 minutes or until golden brown. Drain in the dish lined with kitchen paper. Scatter with salt and serve with some halved lemons.

*This is enough to coat 500 g (1 lb 2 oz) of a mixture or one of the above.*

250 g (9 oz/2 cups) '00' flour or cornflour (corn starch)

200 ml (7 fl oz) water or milk

groundnut or sunflower oil, for frying

Fine salt, to serve

Lemons, halved, to serve

PIZZA ALLA ROMANA

# *Thin Roman Pizza*

SERVES 4

One of the best pizza emporiums in Rome is called Forno Campo de'Fiori, the 'bakery in the flower market', where the long, oval pizzas are freshly baked in their kitchen. The owner, Fabrizio Roscioli, told us that the important thing about making the very flat and crisp *pizza Romana* is that the yeast should be killed quickly in the oven so that the bread doesn't rise any further. It is for this reason he uses bread ovens that are incredibly hot. It is difficult to get anywhere near the temperature needed at home, but you can use a pizza stone, a large ovenproof tile or at least a flat baking sheet (or a baking tray turned upside down) left in the oven to heat. This is our version – with the help of Edoardo Mortari, who makes wonderful Roman pizzas in his restaurant, Arancina, in London – which after much experimentation gets as near as you can to the perfect Roman pizza without the airfare! You won't get the very long pizzas (shown in the photographs overleaf) in a domestic oven, so we have split our dough into four and you can make them round or rectangular as you wish.

## METHOD

Make the dough following the method on page 60. Remove the dough from the fridge and tip it from the bowl, using a dough scraper to loosen it, on to a surface well-floured with semolina. Divide the dough into 4 even-sized pieces using a sharp knife or dough scraper. Make each quarter into a ball, cover in semolina and allow to rest for 40 minutes. While the dough is resting, turn on the oven to its highest heat, which should be somewhere between 250–300°C (480–575°F), with a pizza stone, baking sheet or an upturned baking tray inside.

Make the sauce by mixing all the ingredients together in a bowl. Break up the tomatoes with a potato masher or stick blender until the sauce is smooth. Have a large spoon or ladle ready for pouring it over the pizza base. Prepare your mozzarella and any other toppings now as well.

Flatten the pizza base with your fingertips, creating indentations as you do so. Stretch them out to rectangles or circles around 1 cm (½ in) thick. Make sure there is plenty of semolina underneath so that they don't stick.

Carefully slide one base on to a thin lightly-floured baking sheet or pizza paddle. Make sure the dough can move easily on the surface as you will need to transfer it swiftly from here to the hot oven tray. Push your fingers into the surface of the dough to stretch it out to 5 mm (¼ in) thick and then spread over a thin layer of tomato sauce making sure you don't splash over the edge. Work quickly as the longer you leave it the more chance the pizza has of sticking to the paddle. Scatter over the mozzarella and drizzle over the olive oil then transfer the pizzas to the upturned tray or stone with a tilt and shove. Open and shut the door as quickly as possible so as not to lose any heat. Cook for 8–10 minutes or until the crust is browned in places and the cheese is bubbling. While this pizza is cooking, prepare the next pizza in the same way and repeat the process until all the pizzas are cooked. Remove from the oven and cool on a wire rack for a few minutes before cutting and serving.

500 g (1 lb 2 oz/4 cups)
strong white bread flour

325 ml (11 fl oz) water

10 g ($^1/_2$ oz) coarse organic
salt, plus extra to finish

7 g ($^1/_4$ oz) sugar

3 g ($^1/_8$ oz) beer yeast or
active dried yeast

2 tablespoons
of olive oil

Semolina flour, for
rolling the dough

**FOR THE TOMATO SAUCE
(MAKES ENOUGH FOR 2 LARGE
PIZZAS)**

1 x 400 g (14 oz) tin
Italian plum tomatoes

1 heaped teaspoon
dried oregano

1 teaspoon salt

1 large garlic clove,
finely chopped

2 tablespoons olive oil

**FOR THE TOPPING**

250 g (9 oz) buffalo or cow's
milk mozzarella, roughly torn

50 ml (2 fl oz)
extra-virgin olive oil

CARCIOFI ALLA GIUDIA

# Jewish-style Deep-fried Artichokes

SERVES 4

Our Roman Jewish friend Silvia Nacamulli told me not to even attempt this dish without having the right kind of artichoke. She said they must open like a chrysanthemum and only the less compact versions of the purplish-green Roman artichokes will do this – and they are only around in spring. If you do find them or grow them and want to have a go, you will be rewarded by a real treat. The deep-fried artichokes become like golden sunflowers; the outer leaves having been transformed into salty crisps and the centre into a tender heart.

## METHOD

To prepare the artichokes, first pull off the tough outer leaves. Trim the leaves from the outside inwards with a sharp knife, cutting roughly a third off the top. You can do this with a sharp paring knife, turning the artichoke as you cut, working in a spiral towards the centre and cutting off less as you get to the most tender on the inside. Cut the end off the stalk leaving approximately 5 cm (2 in) still on the artichoke. Cut away the dark tough outer parts of the remaining bit of stalk, exposing the paler inner stalk, and slice off the base scales of the artichoke with a knife. If the artichokes are young, and they should be, there shouldn't be a fluffy choke inside, but if there is remove it with a spoon.

Now gently open out the petals of the artichoke. (This is easier to do under a stream of cold running water.) When you have finished doing this, put the artichoke it in a bowl with enough cold water to cover it. Squeeze in the juice from the lemon to prevent the artichokes from blackening. Continue preparing the rest of the artichokes in the same way.

When you are ready to fry them, remove the artichokes from the water and drain them heads down on some kitchen paper.

Pat them as dry as possible with more kitchen paper.

Fill a large stock or pasta pot with enough oil to deep fry the artichokes in; make sure the pot is deep enough that the oil fills no more than half of the pot as you need to allow room for the artichokes and the oil bubbling up slightly. Alternatively, use a deep-fat fryer if you have one. Heat the oil over a high heat until a small piece of bread sizzles straight away when dropped into the oil. Carefully lower an artichoke into the oil using tongs and push it down so it's fully submerged. Fry until lightly browned. Remove from the oil and drain on kitchen paper, head down. Repeat with the remaining artichokes.

At this point you can leave the artichokes for a few hours if you don't want to eat them straight away. When cool enough to touch with your hands, gently open the leaves a little more. Season them with salt inside and out, and put them back into the fryer. The leaves should open up further and become crispy. Fry until they are deep brown. Remove from the oil and stand on more kitchen paper, heads down, to absorb the oil and serve hot.

4 artichokes

1 lemon

Groundnut or sunflower oil, for frying

Fine salt

POLPETTE DI BOLLITO DI MANZO

# *Beef Patties*

SERVES 8–12 (makes 24–27 golf ball-size patties)

This recipe is from Lucia Ziroli who runs Sora Margherita in the Jewish quarter of Rome where typically the toughest cuts of beef, such as brisket or chuck, are used to great effect. It is boiled for hours resulting in meat that becomes meltingly tender and leaves behind a delicious stock. If you decide to breadcrumb and fry the patties they will have a crunchy coating and the softest meaty centres. Mould them into the size of a small burger and they will make a great lunch with bread and salad, or if made small they are the perfect size to pop in your mouth at a party with drinks. Alternatively, fry them straight after flouring to seal them and then heat through in the broth or a tomato sauce (see *Sugo Finto* on page 137). Sora Margherita is a tiny restaurant with an even tinier kitchen, but the food is big on flavour so do seek it out and book in advance to secure a table. Originally a Jewish recipe like this would not have contained milk or cheese, but we like this adaption.

As a gluten-free alternative to this recipe you can use mashed potato in place of the breadcrumbs. Boil 300 g (10½ oz) of potatoes in their skins until cooked through, scrape the skins off with a knife and put them through a potato ricer or mash straight away. Allow to cool and add in place of the milk-soaked bread. Use rice flour to coat the patties before frying and omit the egg and breadcrumbs.

Sunflower oil, for frying

**TO COOK THE BEEF**

1 kg (2 lb 3 oz) chuck steak or brisket

7 litres (238 fl oz) cold water

2 carrots, peeled and halved

4 celery sticks with leaves

1 onion, skin on and halved, or 1 leek top

3 bay leaves

1 sprig thyme

Few parsley stalks (optional)

**TO MAKE THE PATTIES**

20 g (³/₄ oz) flat-leaf parsley

50 g (2 oz) Parmesan, finely grated

300 g (10 ½ oz) soft bread

400 ml (13 fl oz) milk

1–2 eggs

1 teaspoon salt

**TO COAT THE PATTIES**

Plain (all-purpose) flour for dusting

2 eggs, beaten

50 g (2 oz) fine breadcrumbs

When you are ready to make the patties, heat the frying oil to around 175°C (340°F) in a large high-sided saucepan or a deep-fat fryer. If you are using a pan, make sure you fill it no more than half full with oil. Drain the beef and vegetables from the stock, reserving the stock. (Either freeze this for another day – you can use it for the rich tomato sauce *Sugo Finto* on page 137 or any of the soups – or use it to poach the meatballs, see below.) Discard the vegetables. Cut the meat into manageable pieces through a stand mixer with a mincing attachment and mince into a bowl, or use a food processor to coarsely chop it – do not over blend it into a paste; you want it to look like a rough pâté. Add the remaining ingredients for the patties to the bowl and combine everything together. Fry a small piece of the mixture in a frying pan and taste it to test for the flavour; adjust the seasoning as necessary. When you are happy, make up the rest of the patties by rolling them between your palms to the size of a golf ball, then flatten them to look like small burgers.

To coat the patties, put the flour, beaten eggs and the breadcrumbs into separate bowls. Dip the patties into the flour, then egg and finally the breadcrumbs, then fry for around 5 minutes until cooked through and chestnut brown. Depending on the size of your pan, you may need to do this in batches. Drain on kitchen paper and eat straight away, or cool and reheat in the oven if you want them hot later.

To cook the patties in a broth: Make the beef patties as before. Dip them in flour, shake off the excess, then seal all round in hot seed oil in a frying pan. Gently put the fried patties into the hot beef stock and poach for around 15–20 minutes until cooked through. Serve in warm bowls in the beef broth with a scattering of parsley and grated Parmesan.

SUPPLÌ AL TELEFONO

# Hot Rice Fritters Stuffed with Mozzarella

MAKES 10–12 (large supplì)

In our opinion Arcangelo Dandini makes the best *supplì* in Rome, and we have eaten a few! Breadcrumbed fritters the shape of fat sausages are made out of cheesy, tomato risotto and are filled with mozzarella. As they are served straight from the fryer, melting strings of cheese ooze out of them when they are bitten into resembling Rome's telegraph wires known as *supplì*. Arcangelo's *supplì* were originally made at his more formal restaurant called Ristorante L'Arcangelo, however, they were so popular he opened Supplizio to serve street food such as this and the Mint Frittata in Tomato Sauce on page 50.

He told us that to make his famous *supplì*, the cheese inside needs to reach 140°C (280°F) to melt perfectly.

METHOD

In a large high-sided frying pan, fry the onion in the olive oil, butter, salt and pepper over a medium heat for around 5 minutes until soft and translucent – don't let it become coloured. Add the rice and stir through so that the grains are coated in oil. Pour in the hot stock in one go and bring to the boil. Cook the rice over a medium heat until it is very soft and the liquid has been absorbed. Stir frequently and be careful not to let it catch on the bottom of the pan. Remove from the heat and pour onto a large baking tray to cool. Stir it around frequently to help it to cool down quickly; you want it to cool within an hour to reduce any risk of bacteria.

Once the risotto has reached room temperature, add the tomato sauce and work it into the rice with your hands to break it down until it feels sticky and malleable. Taste and adjust the seasoning as necessary. Form oblong-shaped rice balls with your hands, roughly the size of a large egg. Using your finger make a hole in the centre of each ball and stuff a small cube of mozzarella in the centre. Close the hole over and squeeze tightly between your hands shaping it into a fat sausage shape.

Fill a saucepan with enough sunflower oil to cover the *supplì*, but make sure the oil fills no more than half of the pan. For best results, use a small pan and fry the *supplì* one at a time, but you can use a larger pan and cook several at once too. Heat the oil to 180°C (350°F). Put some flour, the beaten egg and the breadcrumbs each into separate bowls. Dip and gently roll the rice balls first in the flour, then the egg and finally the breadcrumbs to coat all sides. Using a slotted spoon, gently place them in the hot oil in small batches. Fry for 2–3 minutes until crisp and golden brown. Remove with the slotted spoon and drain on kitchen paper for a couple of minutes before serving immediately; the mozzarella should be stringy and melted inside.

1 small white onion,
finely chopped

2 tablespoons
extra-virgin olive oil

25 g (1 oz)
salted butter

Salt and freshly
ground black pepper

400 g (14 oz) risotto rice
(carnaroli or arborio)

1.2 litre homemade hot chicken
or vegetable stock (see page 107)

200 ml (7 fl oz)
*Sugo Finto* tomato sauce
(see page 137), cooled

1 x 125 g (4 oz) mozzarella ball
(buffalo or cow's milk), diced

Sunflower oil,
for frying

Plain (all-purpose) flour,
for dusting

1 medium egg,
lightly beaten

120 g (4 oz)
fine breadcrumbs

# *Soups*

Soups have always been comforting and nourishing but most people don't know why that is. Broth made from tougher cuts of meat or chicken carcasses contains gelatine, which is released into the water as the meat and bones cook; this is what makes a good stock jelly-like in consistency. The gelatine lines your intestine and helps it to mend, encouraging healthy gut flora. This is why the medieval White Chicken and Almond Soup *(see page 104)*, the modern-day chicken soup such as *stracciatella* – called the Jewish penicillin – made with chicken broth and beaten egg, or in my culture beef consommé, were given to the sick; all the while our mothers really did know best, they just didn't know why.

Most soups start with a *soffritto*: a minutely cut, colourful blend of carrot, onion and celery, which is fried in plenty of olive oil until soft. This gives flavour to soups, sauces and stews alike, and can't be beaten. Pasta soups are classic *cucina povera*, poor man's cooking, that kept hunger at bay in bad times, but is now cherished. Paolo from La Campana restaurant told us that the more a society grows in wealth, the more we recognise that the simple things like a good pasta soup are exceptional. We haven't included it here because the ingredients are not readily available, but you will often see *'la minestra della broccoli e arzilla'* on menus in Rome. It a slightly bizarre but delicious soup made from the Romanesco broccoli, skate and pasta. Skate wings and broccoli were commonplace in Italian markets and so were put to good use in this nourishing soup.

VIGNAROLA

# Broad Bean, Artichoke and Pea Stew

SERVES 8-10

Call in the troops or cheat! You have two options here to create this springtime dish. It takes a lot of love and patience to make it from fresh ingredients, so do split the work between friends. We enlisted the help of our passing managing director, Roberto, at work one day; an hour later he was still standing there in the kitchen shelling peas. It did give us a chance to talk though, so perhaps we will start bringing vegetables to our meetings in future! Alternatively, use some frozen or canned vegetables to save time. Traditionally it is made with *guanciale* (a cured meat made from pork cheeks) or pancetta, which is unsmoked, but we also rather like the smoky background flavour of smoked bacon. Some people also shred a lettuce into the dish in the last five minutes of the cooking time and others leave the chilli out. Because this is a stew, the vegetables will lose their vibrant green colour, but it still tastes of spring. Eat it as a starter or main course with crusty bread.

## METHOD

If you are using fresh peas and broad beans still in their pods, remove them from their pods into separate bowls. If you are using whole fresh artichokes, follow the instructions on how to clean and prepare them on page 89, then cut them into quarters and, if they have them, remove the furry chokes in the centre with a spoon.

Sweat the bacon (if using), onion, garlic, chilli and seasoning with the 5 tablespoons of oil in a large saucepan over a medium heat for around 5 minutes until the onion is translucent. Pour in the wine and allow to reduce for a few minutes. Add the hot water and the peas. Cook the peas for around 30 minutes so that they lose their colour but gain sweetness.

While the peas are cooking, in a separate pan, boil the broad beans for 3–5 minutes until just tender, then drain and put them into a bowl of cold water to cool. If you are using

fresh broad beans, remove and discard the tough outer skin of each bean so that you are left with only the bright green centre bean. If you have used the small, young frozen ones that are tender, you shouldn't need to shell them. Cook the fresh or frozen artichokes in a saucepan of boiling salted water for about 10–15 minutes until just tender. Remove and drain but save the cooking liquor if they were fresh. If you are using tinned artichokes, rinse them in cold water to remove the brine and then heat them in a saucepan of boiling water for 3–4 minutes before adding to the peas.

Add the cooked broad beans and artichokes to the pan with the cooked peas, along with 300 ml (10 fl oz) of artichoke water or hot water. Stir and cook everything together over a low heat for 30 minutes. Adjust the seasoning as necessary and serve scattered with the parsley, mint and a swirl of your best extra-virgin olive oil.

1 kg (2 lb 3 oz) peas
in the pod, or 300g
(10$^1$/$_2$ oz) podded
fresh or frozen

1 kg (2 lb 3 oz) broad
(fava) beans in the pod,
or 300 g (10$^1$/$_2$ oz) podded
fresh or frozen

1 kg (2 lb 3 oz) small
artichokes (approx. 8), or
400 g (14oz) frozen or tinned
in brine (drained weight)

50 g (2 oz) smoked or
unsmoked streaky
bacon, pancetta or
*guanciale* (optional)

1 white medium
onion, finely chopped

1 fat garlic clove, peeled
and lightly crushed

1 small dried red
chilli (optional)

Salt and freshly ground
black pepper

5 tablespoons
extra-virgin olive oil

100 ml (3$^1$/$_2$ fl oz) white wine

1 litre (34 fl oz)
hot water

Handful of flat-leaf
parsley, finely chopped

Handful of mint,
finely chopped

Best-quality
extra-virgin olive
oil, to serve

BIANCOMANGIARE

# White Chicken and Almond soup

**SERVES 6–8** (makes 1.5 litres/51 fl oz)

'To prepare a thick white broth with almond milk,' Scappi, the famous Renaissance chef, tells us in his book *Opera*, 'take shelled Milanese almonds and make them into milk with cold lean *capon* broth.' This was a soup often made to nurse the sick back to health, but it was raved about in the Renaissance and the whiter in colour the end result the more it was enjoyed. As food writer Gillian Riley puts it, *Biancomangiare* would have glowed with the luminosity of a full moon among the sombre stews and sauces, the deep browned roasts.' Scappi filtered it to ensure any specks of almond shell or impurities were removed. However, we love it unfiltered with the almond meal left in and believe it does have wonderful nourishing qualities. A good chicken broth will mend the stomach, the protein in the almonds and chicken will regenerate the body, and a dash of verjuice, or in our case lemon, will add vital vitamin C. Somewhere down the historical line this soup must be linked to the Spanish soup *ajo blanco*, a cold soup of almonds and garlic. This can be made out of leftover cold chicken or turkey and, if you must have some colour, accentuate the whiteness with bright red pomegranate seeds.

## METHOD

If you make the chicken stock fresh for this recipe, retain the carcasses from the stock to use again in this recipe. Pour the stock into a medium lidded saucepan and add the chicken breasts (with the reserved carcasses if you have them), cinnamon and bay leaf. Bring the stock to a simmer and poach the chicken for up to 45 minutes until cooked through (the length of time will depend on their size). Remove from the heat and strain the stock into a large jug or bowl. Set aside the chicken to cool.

Put the almonds into a food processor with a little of the stock and blend until smooth (originally this would have been done in a pestle and mortar so do use one of those if you prefer). If you still have the carcasses from the stock, pick the lean chicken off the bones and add it to the food processor along with the poached chicken breasts. Discard the skin and bones. Blend the chicken into the almond mixture until really smooth. Pour into a large clean saucepan and add the rest of the stock. Bring the soup to a gentle boil, stirring occasionally, and add the white pepper and salt to taste. Allow to simmer for 10 minutes then serve in warm bowls with a swirl of lemon juice stirred into each bowl before serving. As Scappi says at the end of his recipe, 'When it is done, serve it hot, on thin slices of bread or not.'

1.5 litres (51 fl oz) homemade chicken stock (see page 107)

2 medium free-range chicken breasts

1 medium cinnamon stick

1 bay leaf

200 g (7 oz) shelled almonds, either whole or flaked, brown skins removed

$1/2$ teaspoon ground white pepper

1–2 teaspoons salt

Juice of $1/2$ lemon

BRODO DI VERDURE

# Vegetable Stock

MAKES 4 LITRES (135 FL OZ)

This has to be the simplest and cheapest stock to make: nothing is fried first and no oil is added. You won't need to buy another stock cube after learning this recipe! It is essential for soups and enhances casseroles and *risotti*. If we are doing a lot of cooking, instead of using whole vegetables we collect peelings from the vegetables listed below during the course of the week, adding them to a plastic food bag in the freezer. When we have collected enough – about 500 g (1 lb 2 oz) – we use them to make this stock.

1 small onion, unpeeled and roughly chopped

1 carrot, cut into 1 cm ($^1/_2$ in) lengths

1 celery heart and 2 celery sticks (or use 4 celery sticks), cut into 1 cm ($^1/_2$ in) lengths

1 leek, washed and cut into 1 cm ($^1/_2$ in) lengths including green tops

1 bay leaf

Handful of parsley stalks

Few sprigs thyme

8 black peppercorns

1 Parmesan rind

2 garlic cloves, unpeeled and crushed

Few sprigs lovage (optional)

$^1/_4$ celeriac, washed and roughly chopped (optional)

5 litres (170 fl oz) water

METHOD

Put all the prepared ingredients into a very large stockpot and add the water. Bring to the boil and reduce to a simmer for 1 hour. Skim any scum from the surface of the stock periodically. Strain the stock into a large bowl or jug, discarding all the vegetables, and use immediately, or leave to cool and refrigerate for up to 4 days. You can also freeze this stock for up to 3 months.

TO MAKE CHICKEN STOCK

For a chicken stock do the same as above but add 2 cooked or raw chicken carcases. Once brought to a boil, skim the surface of any scum. Turn down the heat so that it bubbles gently for around 3 hours. Strain and keep as above.

ZUPPA DI LEGUME

# *Bean and Pasta Soup*

SERVES 6

This is colourful and satisfying peasant fare that dishes out comfort by the ladleful. It is a great way to fill up our hungry teenagers as well as impress guests for lunch. We sometimes use spelt in the soup in place of the pasta as we like the nutty flavour and lower gluten content. This recipe comes from Enoteca Corsi in central Rome; it is a lovely old casual restaurant that has been keeping the locals happy for decades. See photo overleaf.

## METHOD

To make the *soffritto*, finely chop the onion, celery and carrots by hand or in a food processor.

Heat the oil in a large heavy-based saucepan and cook the *soffritto* with the garlic, bay leaves and rosemary over a medium heat for about 15 minutes or until the vegetables are soft – the time will vary depending on their size.

Pour in the wine and allow it to sizzle and reduce, then add the tomatoes and cook for 10 minutes. Stir in the beans, then pour in the stock and bring to a simmer. Leave to cook slowly over a low heat for around 1 hour, adding a little more stock or water if it starts to look dry. Add the pasta about 10 minutes before serving (adjust the time according to the pasta you are using) – don't add it too soon or it will overcook. Remove the Parmesan rind, if you used one, and serve in big warmed bowls dressed with a swirl of your best olive oil.

100 ml ($3^1/_2$ fl oz) extra-virgin olive oil

1 large garlic clove, chopped

2 bay leaves

1 long sprig rosemary

150 ml (5 fl oz) white wine

1 x 400 g (14 oz) tin plum tomatoes

500 g (1 lb 2 oz) tinned mixed beans (drained weight)

1 x 230 g (8 oz) tin cannellini beans

2 litre (68 fl oz) homemade vegetable stock (see page 107 and add the Parmesan rind from the stock)

150 g (5 oz) assorted short pasta or broken spaghetti

3 tablespoons best-quality extra-virgin olive oil, to serve

### FOR THE SOFFRITTO

150 g (5 oz) onion

150 g (5 oz) celery

150 g (5 oz) carrots

MINESTRONE DI VERDURE

# *Minestrone of Vegetables*

SERVES 6–8

I love this nourishing and easy soup from our friends at restaurant Enoteca Corsi in Rome. Its glorious colours sing to you of health and comfort. See photo overleaf.

METHOD

In a large saucepan, fry the onion and potatoes over a medium heat in the olive oil for about 5 minutes until the onion has softened. Pour in the wine and allow it to evaporate for a few minutes while stirring. Add the peas, celery and carrots, and stir through for around 5 minutes before adding the tomatoes, water or stock and salt. Bring to the boil and add the cauliflower and courgettes.

Let the soup simmer for around 40 minutes or until the vegetables are soft. Taste and adjust the seasoning as necessary. Serve in warm bowls with a swirl of your best olive oil and twist of black pepper.

1 medium white onion, finely chopped

2 medium potatoes, peeled and cut into 2 cm (³/₄ in) cubes

3 tablespoons extra-virgin olive oil

3 tablespoons white wine

200 g (7 oz) peas, frozen or fresh

2 celery sticks, cut into 1.5 cm (¹/₂ in) lengths

2 carrots, peeled and cut into 1.5 cm (¹/₂ in) cubes

2 round tomatoes, roughly chopped

1 litre (34 fl oz) water, or homemade vegetable or chicken stock (see page 107)

2 level teaspoons fine salt

1 medium cauliflower, cut into small bite-size florets

2 courgettes (zucchinis), cut into 1.5 cm (¹/₂ in) thick circles

Best-quality extra-virgin olive oil, to serve

Freshly ground black pepper

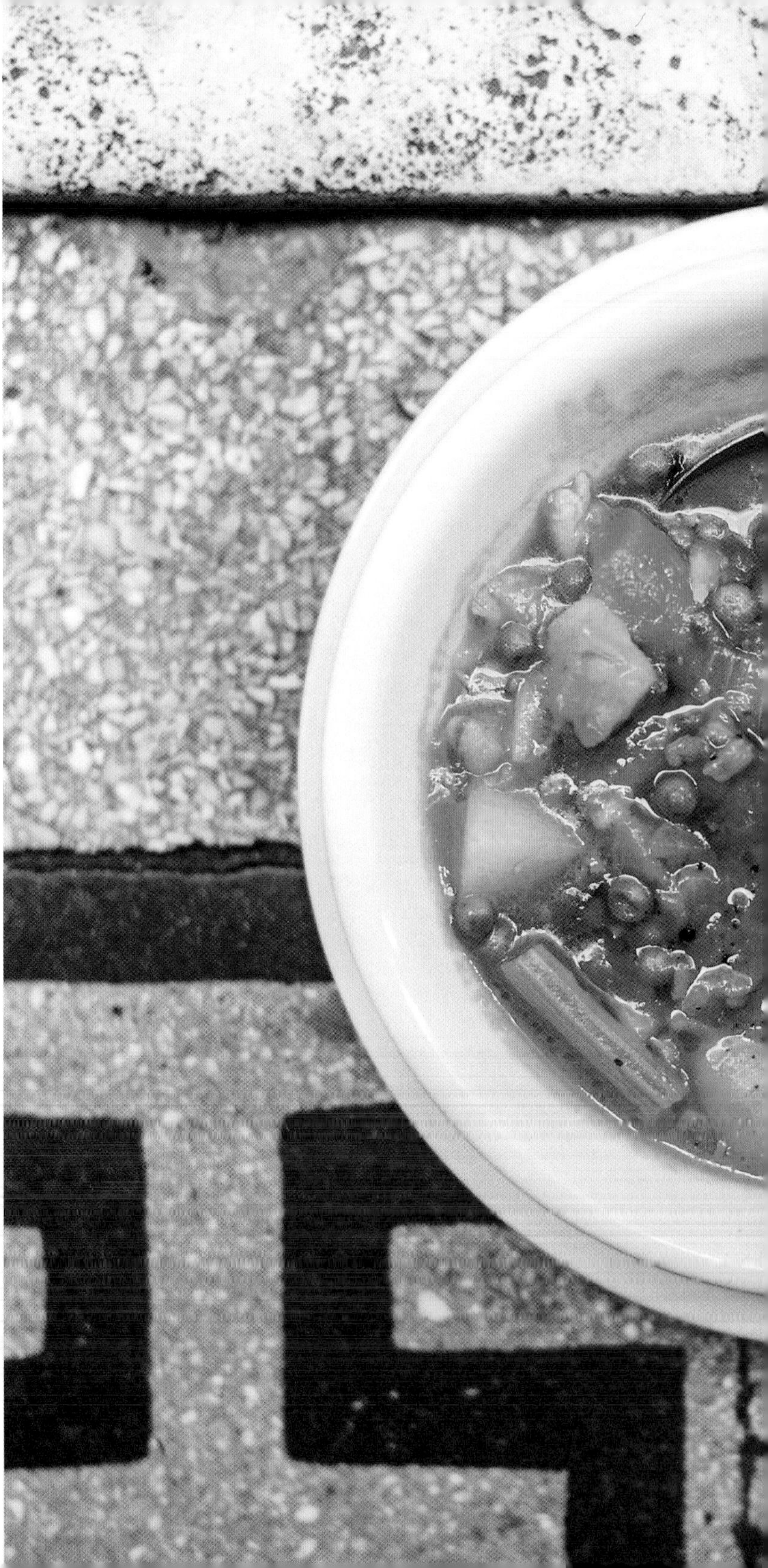

MINESTRONE OF VEGETABLES,
PAGE 111

BEAN & PASTA SOUP,
PAGE 110

ZUPPA DI CECI

# Chickpea Soup

SERVES 8–10

Tuesday is chickpea soup day in Rome. It has been like this for centuries as Tuesday, like Friday, was a fasting day in the Catholic church and meat was forbidden. Often it is topped with baby octopus called *moscardini*, which are easily available in Italy but not here in the UK, so instead we have used crispy fried onions. We have used a *soffritto*, as it adds a wonderful herby base flavour. If you find the chickpea a little hard, do add a teaspoon of bicarbonate of soda ten minutes before the end of the cooking time to soften them. We tend to purée a third of the chickpeas and leave the rest whole so you can squash them in your mouth and reveal their soft interiors. Often this soup has pasta cooked in it for the last few minutes of the cooking time. If you are going to do that, remove a third of the chickpeas to purée, add the pasta and cook it through, then put the puréed chickpeas back into the soup to thicken it. You may also need to add a little extra stock because the pasta absorbs a lot of liquid.

## METHOD

Make a *soffritto* by finely chopping the carrot, celery and onions. Heat the 7 tablespoons of oil in a large heavy-based saucepan over a medium heat and add the *soffritto* with the anchovies, if using, garlic, bay leaves, sage and rosemary. Cook for around 15 minutes, depending on the size of the vegetables, until soft. Drain and wash the chickpeas and add to the pan. Stir through so they become coated in the oil from the *soffritto*. Add the tomato purée and seasoning and stir again. Now add the stock or water and the Parmesan rind, and bring to the boil. Reduce to a simmer and continue to cook for around 1 hour 30 minutes to 2 hours or until the chickpeas are tender and soft. Add the bicarbonate of soda if the chickpeas still have tough skins after 2 hours and continue to simmer for a further 10 minutes.

Meanwhile make the crispy onions. Fry the onions in a large frying pan in the sunflower oil over a medium-high heat until crispy. Remove from the pan and drain on kitchen paper. Scatter with salt to taste.

Remove and discard the rosemary and bay leaves from the soup. Transfer about a third of the soup to a food processor and blend until smooth, or use a large bowl and a stick blender. Pour the blended soup back into the pan and stir through. Serve in warm bowls with a drizzle of good extra-virgin olive oil, a few crisp onions and a shower of grated Parmesan.

7 tablespoons extra-
virgin olive oil

2 tinned anchovy fillets
in oil (optional)

2 fat garlic cloves,
peeled and lightly crushed

2 bay leaves

Sprig sage leaves

Sprig rosemary

500 g (1 lb 2 oz)
chickpeas, soaked
overnight in cold water

2 heaped tablespoons
tomato purée (paste)

2.2 litres (75 fl oz) homemade
chicken or vegetable stock
(see page 107) or water

1 Parmesan rind

1 teaspoon bicarbonate
of soda (if necessary)

Salt and freshly ground
black pepper

Best-quality extra-virgin
olive oil, to serve

25 g (1 oz) Parmesan,
finely grated, to serve

**FOR THE *SOFFRITTO***

1 large carrot

3 celery sticks

2 medium white onions

**FOR THE CRISPY ONIONS**

1 medium white onion, finely
sliced into semi-circles

Sunflower oil, for frying

Salt

# *Pasta & Gnocchi*

There is no better visual to display the feeling of national culinary pride than the photograph from the film *An American in Rome* with Alberto Sordi stuffing his mouth with pasta. As a boy, Sordi's character wanted to like everything American including the food. In this famous scene, he tries to eat a meal made of milk, jam, yoghurt, mustard and mayonnaise, all the time singing the praises of the American way of life, but finally rejects it in favour of his mother's irresistible macaroni.

Fresh pasta is made in Rome, such as the fresh square-cut *tonnarelli*, *fettuccine* and parcels of ricotta and spinach, but it is what they do with the dried pasta that impresses the most.

On one of our summer visits, straight from the plane, we went to La Campana for lunch for our fix of pasta. Simple combinations like fresh anchovy and dried red chilli, cheese and black pepper, and *la gricia* made with cured ham and cheese, is to us the best of Roman pasta. Come for the carbonara and see how it is really done, with no cream in sight.

SPAGHETTI 'AJO E OJO'

# Spaghetti with Garlic, Parsley and Chilli

SERVES 4

This bowlful of garlicky, spicy head-tingling pasta has to be miles better than any processed food you can prepare in ten minutes. Giancarlo and his friends used to eat this after a late night working at the Rome Hilton, or even in the early hours of the morning after a night's dancing as it was quick to prepare and they always had the ingredients in the house. Its simplicity is the key to its success through generations of Italians and is summed up by the Roman proverb '*pui si penne, peggio si mangia*': 'The more you put in, the worse you eat.'

## METHOD

Cook the spaghetti in a large saucepan of well-salted, boiling water according to the packet instructions until al dente. While the pasta is cooking, heat the oil in a large frying pan over a medium heat and gently fry the garlic, chilli (add more or less according to your taste), salt and pepper for 2 minutes maximum without letting it colour. Drain the spaghetti and throw it into the frying pan with the parsley and toss to combine. Serve in warm bowls sprinkled with the cheese.

320 g (11$^1$/$_2$ oz) spaghetti

8 tablespoons
good extra-virgin olive oil

1 fat garlic clove, peeled
and finely chopped

1 dried or fresh red chilli,
finely chopped, to taste

Salt and freshly ground
black pepper

20 g ($^3$/$_4$ oz)
flat-leaf parsley,
finely chopped

50 g (2 oz) pecorino or
Parmesan, finely grated

SPAGHETTI 'AJO', 'OJO', MENTA, SCAMPI E LIMONE

# Spaghetti with Garlic, Oil, Prawns, Lemon and Mint

**SERVES 4** (as a main and 6 as a starter)

This is restaurant Pierluigi's twist on the classic *Spaghetti Ajo e Ojo* on page 120. Plump pink scampi are tossed with lemon zest and mint leaves to create a joy to look at and a delight to eat. If you can, try to find whole prawns with their heads still on; the flavour with be far superior to those without.

### METHOD

Peel the shells off the prawns but leave the heads intact: the flavour lies within. Use the pointed tip of a small knife to remove the black vein from the backs of the prawns. Cook the spaghetti in a large saucepan of well-salted boiling water according to the packet instructions until al dente. Halfway through the cooking time for the spaghetti, heat the oil in a large frying pan over a medium-high heat and sauté the prawns and garlic for around 5 minutes or until the prawns turn pink and are cooked through. Add the wine and allow to reduce for a few minutes. Add the butter and stir through. Drain the spaghetti and toss it in the pan with the herbs and lemon zest to combine with the sauce.

360 g (12$^1$/$_2$ oz) raw shell-on tiger prawns

320 g (11$^1$/$_2$ oz) spaghetti

3 tablespoons extra-virgin olive oil

1 fat garlic clove, finely chopped

4 tablespoons white wine

25 g (1 oz) salted butter

2 tablespoons finely chopped flat-leaf parsley, including thin stalks

Few mint leaves, finely chopped

1 teaspoon finely grated lemon zest

Fine salt

RIGATONI I ALL'AMATRICIANA

# Pasta with Tomato, Bacon and Onion Sauce

SERVES 6

*Bucatini*, in the photo, is one of the silliest forms of pasta ever made. It is thick and difficult to wrap around your fork, whips around your face as you suck it in and whistles as the air passes through it almost so as to draw attention to your lack of finesse. It also splashes its bright red coating of sauce around your person and clothes. No thank you. Give me good old rigatoni or penne any day. However, a well-made *amatriciana* sauce is something to write home about. *Guanciale*, or cured pig's cheeks, is the background meaty flavour imparted by the layers of fat and meat in a cheek that has been coated in pepper and hung in a curing cabinet for months. This renders the *guanciale* sweet, firm to slice and with a kick of umami that is not delivered by the modern slice of mass-produced bacon. If you can't find this, or indeed proper pancetta, buy the best unsmoked streaky, fatty bacon you can.

'*Amatriciana*' comes from Amatrice, a town in the mountainous region of Lazio. This area was Abruzzo before Mussolini changed the border lines. Apparently, this dish originally derives from the mountain people who lived there, who called it *la gricia*, which in those days was simply fried *guanciale*, pasta, black pepper and pecorino, sometimes with a dash of vinegar. Tomatoes were a later addition by the wealthier people of the area who could afford them, and it then became known as *amatriciana*.

5 tablespoons extra-virgin olive oil

500 g (1 lb 2 oz) white onion, finely sliced into semi-circles

250 g (9 oz) *guanciale*, pancetta or streaky bacon, cut into 5 mm (1/4 in) strips

Salt and freshly ground black pepper

100 ml (3 1/2 fl oz) white wine

2 x 400 g (14 oz) tins good-quality plum tomatoes, crushed with your hands

500 g (1 lb 2 oz) rigatoni

50 g (2 oz) Pecorino Romano or Parmesan, finely grated

METHOD

Heat the oil in a large frying pan and fry the onion, *guanciale*, salt and pepper for around 10 minutes until the onion has softened. Add the wine and allow to reduce for about 5 minutes, then add the crushed tomatoes and cook over a gentle simmer for 30 minutes until the sauce reduces and thickens. About 10 minutes before you are ready to serve, cook the pasta in a large pan of salted boiling water according to the packet instructions until al dente. Adjust the seasoning in the sauce as necessary and serve tossed with the drained hot pasta and cheese.

PASTA 'ALLA CHECCA' DI KATIE E GIANCARLO

# *Pasta with 'Raw Sauce'*

SERVES 4 (as a main and 6 as a starter)

This rainbow in a bowl is Rome's celebration of summer. Bright red cherry tomatoes are tossed with capers, olives, basil, mozzarella, chilli and garlic, and finished with ricotta. I like the raw sauce, '*checca*', served with hot spaghetti but it is often served cold stirred into cooled penne for a gorgeous salad.

### METHOD

Cook the spaghetti in a large saucepan of well-salted, boiling water according to the packet instructions until al dente. Meanwhile, gently mix the tomatoes, garlic, capers, olives, chilli and oil together in a bowl. Warm a large mixing bowl ready to toss the spaghetti in. Drain the spaghetti and toss it in the warm bowl with the tomato mixture, season well and then gently mix in the herbs and mozzarella. Serve with spoonfuls of ricotta on top.

320 g (11$^1$/$_2$ oz) spaghetti

200 g (7 oz) cherry tomatoes, halved

1 garlic clove, peeled and finely chopped

20 g ($^3$/$_4$ oz) capers, rinsed well

100 g (3$^1$/$_2$ oz) whole green olives, stones removed and quartered

1 red chilli, finely chopped

5 tablespoons extra-virgin olive oil

Salt and freshly ground black pepper

125 g (4 oz) mozzarella, cut into approx. 2 cm ($^3$/$_4$ in) cubes

3 tablespoons finely chopped flat-leaf parsley, plus extra leaves, to serve

Handful of basil leaves

100 g (3$^1$/$_2$ oz) ricotta

GNOCCHI ALLA ROMANA

# *Semolina Gnocchi*

SERVES 6

This is a particularly Roman way of making gnocchi without a potato in sight. It is a rediscovery in our house since writing the recipe for this book. I have to say I thought it was going to be heavy and rather dismissed it. Giancarlo and the boys loved it, but when we made it for the book photoshoot it was the women in our crew who succumbed to the dark side. Now I am a convert and very happy to spread the word about the warm, crispy, cheesy delights of semolina gnocchi.

## METHOD

Heat the oven to 180°C (350°F/Gas 6). Butter a baking tray measuring around 40 x 30 cm (16 x 12 in) and at least 2 cm (¾ in) deep and have it ready at your side – you will need to pour the semolina into it quickly before it starts to set. In a large saucepan, bring the milk to the boil with the salt, then slowly sprinkle in the sieved semolina stirring constantly with a whisk. When it starts to thicken remove the pan from the heat. Keep whisking the semolina off the heat to stop it becoming lumpy; add 100 g (3¹/₂ oz) of the butter and whisk until fully incorporated. Add half of the Parmesan, both the beaten egg yolks and whisk again. Remember to work quickly as you don't want it to set in the pan. Pour into the buttered oven

tray. Put a layer of baking parchment over the top of the semolina and smooth it down into a flat layer around 2 cm (¾ in) deep. Leave to cool and set. It will take around 1 hour in a cool room.

Meanwhile, generously butter an oven dish measuring around 20 x 30 cm (8 x 12 in) big. When the semolina has cooled and set firm use a 6 cm (2½ in) cutter (or wine glass) to cut out circles. The trimmings can be compacted together and cut out too so nothing is wasted. Lay the circles into the buttered dish and top with flecks of the remaining butter. Scatter over the rest of the cheese. Cook in the oven for around 20 minutes until browned and bubbling hot. Serve on its own.

150 g (5 oz)
salted butter

1 litre
(34 fl oz) milk

1 teaspoon salt

250 g (9 oz/2 cups)
fine semolina,
sieved

100 g (3¹/₂ oz)
Parmesan,
finely grated

2 egg yolks,
beaten

GNOCCHI DI PATATE IN SUGO FINTO

# Potato Gnocchi in Tomato Sauce

SERVES 6

One Thursday we visited restaurant Sora Margherita in the Jewish quarter of Rome where the staff were busy making hundreds of potato gnocchi; it was 'gnocchi Giovedì', or 'gnocchi Thursday'. In Rome, many restaurants follow the tradition of serving certain dishes on specific days, and Thursdays are for gnocchi. These gnocchi are perfect served with the oxtail sauce from *Coda di Vaccinara* on page 184, *Arrabiata* on page 141 or with the *Sugo Finto* on page 137. This gnocchi recipe is from our book *Venice: Recipes Lost and Found*.

Potatoes that are neither too floury nor too waxy are best for making gnocchi. Gnocchi also freeze really well and should be frozen before cooking. This can sometimes give a lighter result, so consider doubling the quantities and freezing half to use another time. To freeze, spread the gnocchi out on a well-floured tray so that they are not touching and pop in the freezer. When they have frozen, shake off the excess flour and transfer them to freezer bags; seal and put back in the freezer. Use them within three months and allow one to two minutes extra cooking time when you come to use them.

METHOD

In a large saucepan, boil the potatoes in their skins in plenty of salted water for around an hour or until tender. Although this takes longer than boiling peeled chopped potatoes, the flavour is far superior as the potatoes don't become watery when protected by their skins. Drain and peel them while they are still hot; use a fork to steady the potato and then peel the skin away with a sharp knife. Pass the potatoes through a potato ricer or food mill on to a wooden board. Add the seasoning and the flour, then the egg and knead together to form a soft, pliable dough.

Bring a large pan of well-salted water to the boil. Lightly flour your work surface. Roll an apple-sized piece of dough into a 2 cm (¾ in) thick length. Cut into 2 cm (¾in) long pieces with a sharp knife, flicking the gnocchi to one side as you cut them. Repeat until all the dough is used. Cook the gnocchi in batches so they aren't crowded in the pan. Drop them into the boiling water and cook for about 2 minutes; they will float to the surface when they are done. Lift them out gently using a slotted spoon and toss them in your warmed chosen sauce.

1 kg (2 lb 3 oz) floury potatoes, such as King Edward, Maris Piper or Desiree

1 heaped teaspoon salt

Generous twist black pepper

300 g (10$^1$/$_2$ oz/ 2$^1$/$_2$ cups) '00' flour, plus extra for dusting

1 egg

1 quantity tomato sauce of your choice (see pages 136–41)

CARBONARA DI ROSCIOLI

# Roscioli's Carbonara

SERVES 4

I have eaten a lot of carbonara in Rome in the name of perfecting this recipe, so I hope my larger dress size is worth it! Some have been too cloying, others are bland, a few tasted of cinnamon (a coating used on some cured meats) and many are served with chewy *guanciale*, the cured, fatty pork cheek that gives this dish its flavour. The best carbonara in Rome that we found was at Roscioli followed by a close second at Felice in Testaccio. It might be because it's a deli and restaurant that Roscioli have the best *guanciale* – they use unusual crushed peppercorns and bright yellow eggs from corn-fed chickens – but I think it's in their cooking.

Equally perfect bowls of this famous pasta can be made at home with pancetta or good-quality streaky bacon, thickly sliced from a good butcher. Make sure it is fatty and for extra flavour use a tablespoon of rendered pork fat (see page 15). Alessandro Roscioli uses an iron frying pan to crisp up the cubes of *guanciale* so that they are crunchy on the outside and soft on the inside; they become like the best pork scratchings you have ever munched on, all combined with pasta in a peppery cheese coating. Incidentally, carbonara is named after the *carbonari*: the charcoal men who fed themselves on the cured meat, cheese and pasta they carried with them into the forest. Presumably black specks of charcoal gave it extra flavour although now they are replaced with pepper.

## METHOD

Cut the *guanciale* or bacon into 1 cm (½ in) cubes. Put them into a frying pan with the fat, if using (if you are using *guanciale* you won't need any extra fat), over a low heat for around 15–20 minutes or until each piece crisps up and releases its fat. Remove from the heat and set aside.

Cook the spaghetti in a large pan of well-salted boiling water until al dente. While the pasta is cooking, beat the egg yolks and white together in a large bowl. Add the salt, pepper and 125 g (2 oz) of the cheese. Once the pasta is cooked, put back into the saucepan. Add the bacon and fat and stir through with a wooden spoon. Continue stirring while adding the cheese and egg mixture. Serve straight away in hot bowls scattered with the remaining cheese. Tell your guests to eat it up as soon as they get it. As Giancarlo says, 'Pasta waits for no man.'

250 g (9 oz) *guanciale*,
or unsmoked rindless pancetta
or streaky bacon plus 2
tablespoons pork fat or olive oil

320 g (11¹/₂ oz) spaghetti

3 large egg yolks

1 egg

Good pinch of salt

1 teaspoon freshly ground
Sarawak, Sichuan
or black pepper

150 g (5 oz) Pecorino Romano
or Parmigiano Reggiano,
finely grated

CACIO E PEPE

# Cheese and Pepper Pasta

SERVES 4

There are many ways to make this classic dish and each Roman cook will show you some slightly different way to manipulate pasta, cheese and pepper into a wonderful, warm bowl of comfort food. We saw this method, called 'risotato' as it is like making a risotto, being used by chef Rossana Gialleonardo at Il Casaletto restaurant in the surrounding hills of Rome. After sharing her trick with us, we sat down to eat the creamiest version of *Cacio e Pepe* ever and decided from now on that is how we would do it. The pasta is cooked in a frying pan and the cooking water reduces and reduces to become the sauce. The typical Roman pasta to use for this dish is fresh *tonnarelli*, a sort of squared spaghetti, but for this method spaghetti is a must. The cheese should be the semi-soft sheep's cheese from Lazio, called *Cacio de Roma*, but if you find this hard to find use Pecorino Romano or Parmigiano Reggiano instead.

METHOD

Heat the oil with the pepper in a large frying pan (around 30 cm/12 in) over a medium heat until hot and you can smell the heady spice of the pepper. Put the spaghetti into the frying pan and add 1 litre of the hot water, little by little, and the salt. Stir frequently and cook for around 10 minutes. While the pasta is cooking, warm some bowls in a low oven. If the pasta starts to look dry, add a little more water. When the water has reduced to a soupy consistency and the pasta is al dente remove the pan from the heat and add the cheese a little at a time, stirring furiously. Serve straight away in hot bowls – this is important to prevent the cheese from setting.

3 tablespoons extra-virgin olive oil

1 level teaspoon freshly ground black pepper

320 g (11¹/₂ oz) *tonnarelli* or spaghetti

1–1.2 litres (34–41 fl oz) boiling water

Generous pinch of salt

100 g (3¹/₂ oz) *Cacio de Roma* or Pecorino Romano or Parmigiano Reggiano, grated

SUGO FINTO

# Roman Tomato Sauce

SERVES 6

This is so called as originally it was (and can still be) made with pork fat and meat stock, but doesn't contain any actual meat so it is a false or '*finto*' meat sauce. It is delicious in this way but if you don't have small amounts of fat and stock lying around it is just as delicious without. This make a rough-textured sauce but equally it can be put it through a *passatutto* (food mill) or blended with a stick blender to make it smooth and velvety. It turns quite bright orange in colour when blended and it's very pretty on pasta or as a soup, decorated with basil leaves and Parmesan shavings – see page 140 for Flavio's Tomato and Pasta Soup.

METHOD

Finely chop the celery, onion and carrot by hand or in a food processor, taking care that the pieces are small – even tiny – but not puréed, to make a *soffritto*. Heat the oil in a medium saucepan and add the *soffritto*. Fry over a medium heat for about 10–15 minutes until soft. Add the garlic, herbs (if using) and salt and pepper, and fry for 1 minute to soften the garlic. Add the tomatoes and use a potato masher to mash them down. Wash each of the tins out with the water or meat stock and add this to the saucepan. Heat the tomatoes until they start to bubble then turn the heat down to a simmer and leave the sauce to cook for around 30–40 minutes, stirring frequently. Remove the herbs. Taste the sauce and add more seasoning if necessary; the sauce should be sweet from the carrots and balanced well with the salt and pepper.

6 tablespoons extra-virgin olive oil or rendered pork fat (see page 15)

1 garlic clove, finely chopped

large sprigs basil and parsley (optional)

Salt and freshly ground black pepper

3 x 400 g (14 oz) tins whole plum or cherry tomatoes

200 ml (7 fl oz) water or meat stock (optional)

FOR THE *SOFFRITTO*

1 celery stick

1 medium white or red onion

1 carrot

ZUPPA DI POMODORO ALLA FLAVIO

# Flavio's Tomato and Pasta Soup

To make the *Sugo Finto* (see page 137) into a soup for 4 people, add a 700 ml (24 fl oz) hot vegetable, chicken or meat stock or water to 500 ml (17 fl oz) of the sauce in a large saucepan. Bring to the boil and add 150 g (5 oz) of small pasta shapes such as *farfalline, stelline* or *ditalini*; stir well as they can stick to the bottom of the pan. Continue to cook over a medium heat for 5–6 minutes until the pasta is done. Check the seasoning before serving as it may need a little more salt and pepper to make up for the extra liquid. Serve in warm bowls swirled with good extra-virgin olive oil, black pepper and Parmesan. If you like it spicy, stir some crushed dried chilli into the soup as it cooks, to your taste. Flavio, who is our son, likes his special touch of a down-turned basil leaf on top. Who knows why, there's nowt as strange as kids!

PENNE ALL'ARRABBIATA DA TEO

# *Penne with Spicy Tomato Sauce*

SERVES 4

GUEST RECIPE
*Teo Filippini*
GUEST RECIPE

Da Teo is a typical Roman trattoria owned and run by Teo and his wife. We came to eat here with the children and were excited to try his Roman fayre as the restaurant came highly recommended by Roman friends. The kids spotted *penne arrabbiata* on the menu and insisted on both ordering it. So much for trying a variety of dishes, dipping a fork into each other's and experiencing new flavours and ingredients. We probably eat this once a week at home! However here the sauce was excellent; it was thick, spicy and clung to the pasta. Teo also serves it on potato gnocchi on Thursdays, which is traditionally gnocchi day in Rome. We liked his idea of combining tinned plum tomatoes with sweet cherry tomatoes. As ours at home are not always sun ripened, we have added onions to the sauce as we like the sweetness they offer.

## METHOD

Fry the onion, chilli and garlic in the olive oil in a large frying pan over a medium heat for around 10 minutes or until the onions are soft. Add the tinned tomatoes, salt and pepper, and mash down with a potato masher. Bring to the boil, then lower the heat so that the sauce is just bubbling. Leave to cook for around 30 minutes, stirring occasionally. Boil the pasta in a large saucepan of well-salted water according to the packet instructions until al dente. Add the cherry tomatoes to the sauce and stir through. Drain the pasta and stir it into the sauce to combine. Serve straight away scattered with Parmesan.

1 medium white onion, finely chopped

1 red chilli, finely sliced

2 garlic cloves, peeled and each cut into 3 pieces

5 tablespoons best-quality extra-virgin olive oil

2 x 400 g (14 oz) tins plum or cherry tomatoes

1 teaspoon fine salt

generous twist of freshly ground black pepper

320 g (11½ oz) penne or rigatoni

Handful of fresh ripe flavourful cherry tomatoes

50 g (2 oz) finely grated Parmesan

# Fish & Seafood

Fish is cooked very simply in Rome as elsewhere in Italy, but, lovely though that is, it doesn't make a good recipe; 'First take your fish, grill it, then eat it,' if you see what we mean. One thing is certain, the Romans do insist on it being fresh. Our guide around the market at Ponte Milvio in northern Rome was Wendy Holloway, who has lived in Rome more than 30 years, and pointed out to us the labels on fish counter. They will tell you the Latin name of the species, when and in what zone it was fished, and when and if it was frozen. Italians are aware of the issue of mercury in fish and many won't touch certain types.

Obviously fresh fish must have been a priority for the ancient Romans too, such as General Lucullus. Apparently he wasn't recognised for one of his victories in 66 BC and the Senate refused to give him a triumph (the victory parade through Rome that was every general's ambition) because his great rival Pompey kept blocking it. Instead he devoted all his attention and vast riches to his estate near Naples, and built lavish fishponds fed by a channel directly from the sea to provide seawater so that he could enjoy the freshest seawater fish. This set a trend and, despite the cost, seawater ponds became fashionable in aristocrats' villas along the coast.

Wendy also told us that anchovies were the secret of Rome's cooking. Their appeal has lasted for thousands of years. Perhaps it is the umami hit that they deliver to pep up many other flavours; a natural flavour enhancer that makes them stand the test of time. You will find them snuck into broccoli, soups and sauces, and especially with roast lamb. In ancient Roman days they were made into *garum*, a strong fish sauce that seems to have been added to just about everything.

Our friend Isabella told us not to disregard the fish restaurants along the seafront in Fiumicino as just aimed at tourists and actually we have now had some great meals there with a wonderful view of the sea.

We have picked the best, most doable, recipes we came across on our visits to Rome. You will see that they are simple with few ingredients so the flavour of the fish will not be overwhelmed.

SALTIMBOCCA DI SPIGOLA

# Sea Bass with Parma Ham and Sage Leaves

SERVES 4

This is another of our friend Stefania's 'supper in three ingredients' recipes. She likes to have everything ready around her, including a side dish of potatoes or Green Beans with Lemon (see page 39), as it is a quick dish to cook.

8 small skin-on sea bass or sea bream fillets (approx. 180 g/6 oz each)

Salt and freshly ground black pepper

4 slices prosciutto

8 large sage leaves

Plain (all-purpose) or '00' flour for dusting

2 tablespoons olive oil

50 ml (2 fl oz) white wine

30 g (1 oz) salted butter

## METHOD

Season both sides of the fish. Cut the prosciutto in half widthways so you have 8 slices. Lay a slice of prosciutto and a sage leaf on top of the skinless side of the fish and fix them into place with a toothpick. Repeat this for each fillet. Put some flour into a bowl and dust each piece of fish in flour; shake off the excess and put them on a plate.

Heat the oil in a large non-stick frying pan. Fry the fish prosciutto-side down for 2 minutes and then turn over when just browned. Fry skin side down for another 3–4 minutes or until the fish is cooked through. Add the wine and allow to evaporate. Stir in the butter to thicken the sauce. Remove from the heat and serve the fish straight away drizzled with the sauce.

POLPETTINE DI PESCE IN SUGO DI POMODORO

# Fish Balls and Tomato Sauce

**SERVES 6** (as a starter or 4 as a main)

At the glamorous Pierluigi restaurant in Rome these delightfully soft balls of fish, basil and cheese in a tomato sauce make a sumptuous starter. They use amberjack but you could use any white fish such as cod, haddock or coley.

## METHOD

First make the tomato sauce. Heat the oil in a large saucepan over a medium-high heat and, when hot, add the garlic and herbs. Swirl around the oil with the flavourings for a couple of minutes and then add the tomatoes. Mash them to a pulp with a potato masher, then bring to the boil. Turn the heat down and let the sauce cook for 10–20 minutes while you prepare the fish balls.

Mix together all the ingredients for the fish balls in a bowl by hand. When well combined, roll a small amount into a ball around the size of a walnut. Whenever you make any patty, fish or meat ball always test one first for seasoning. It is awful to make all the shapes and then find when you sit down to eat that actually all it needed was a little more salt or cheese. Heat a little oil in a small frying pan and fry one ball to cook it through – about 5 minutes. You can speed this up by flattening the ball to allow the heat to penetrate more quickly. Taste and make sure you are happy with the seasoning and flavour, adding more seasoning and/or cheese if necessary. Make up the rest of the balls.

Gently place the balls into the tomato sauce to cook for around 10 minutes or until they are cooked through. Remove the sprigs of herbs and serve in warm bowls with crusty bread to mop up the sauce.

## FOR THE TOMATO SAUCE

3 tablespoons extra-virgin olive oil

1 garlic clove, peeled and lightly crushed

1 sprig basil

1 sprig flat-leaf parsley

$1/2$ teaspoon dried oregano

2 x 400 g (14 oz) tins plum tomatoes

## FOR THE FISH BALLS

500 g (1lb 2 oz) coley and cod mixture, minced in a food processor or finely chopped by hand

10 g ($1/2$ oz) basil leaves

1 garlic clove, finely chopped

40 g ($1^1/_2$ oz) Parmigiano Reggiano, finely grated

40 g ($1^1/_2$ oz) stale breadcrumbs

100 ml ($3^1/_2$ fl oz) milk

Finely grated zest of $1/2$ lemon

1 egg yolk

Salt and freshly ground black pepper

PASTICCIO

# *Anna's Sardine Bake*

SERVES 6 (as a starter or 4 as a main)

'That's a fine *pasticcio* you got me into,' one Roman might say to another. It is the name given to dishes made up of jumbled up ingredients, in this case it is sardines, herbs and breadcrumbs, and it is made by our friend Anna Davies, a Roman resident since her youth when she moved to Rome as a dancer. Anna has championed her versions of Roman classics for her family that can be made quickly and suit all tastes. I love this combination of sweet onions, salty fish and crunchy breadcrumbs, and it's become one of our family favourites back home.

## METHOD

Wash, scale and gut the fish, removing their heads, fins and spines. Open them out like a butterfly and pat dry. Set aside. Heat the oven to 180°C (350°F/Gas 6). Fry the onions over a low heat in the oil with the seasoning for around 5 minutes until just soft but not coloured. Remove from the heat when they are done.

In a large bowl, soak the bread in the milk for a couple of minutes, then squeeze out the milk gently breaking up the bread into small pieces; set aside. In an ovenproof dish measuring around 30 x 20 cm (12 x 8 in) layer a third of the onions onto the base. Scatter over a third of the bread, parsley and garlic. Put a third of the sardines on top and season well. Squeeze over a little of the lemon juice and a drizzle of olive oil. Repeat for 2 more layers finishing with the breadcrumbs.

Bake for 15 minutes or until the fish is cooked through and the top is crusty and golden brown. Serve warm with a green salad or Green Beans with Lemon (see page 39).

500 g (1 lb 2 oz) fresh sardines

1 white onion, finely sliced into semi-circles

4 tablespoons extra-virgin olive oil, plus extra for drizzling

100 g (3 1/2 oz) slightly stale white crusty bread

200 ml (7 fl oz) milk

3 tablespoons roughly chopped flat leaf parsley

2 garlic cloves, finely chopped

Salt and freshly ground black pepper

Juice of 1 lemon

PESCE IN CARTOCCIO CON FINOCCHIO SELVATICO

# *Fish and Bronze Fennel in a Parcel*

SERVES 4

Whispery fronds of bronze or green fennel grow in the UK as well as Italy but we don't seem to recognise it here for the fantastic flavour it gives. In Italy they use the stalks, leaves, flowers and seeds, and have done for centuries. It is seen as often in hedgerows as established gardens. If you can't find it use its relative, dill, instead. We have made this with cod but actually any white fish or salmon will work with the fennel.

METHOD

Heat the oven to 180°C (350°F/Gas 6). Cut 4 pieces of baking parchment large enough to fit each fillet in and allowing enough to wrap over the fish and fold up at the edges to make a parcel. Bash the stems of the wild fennel with the flat of a knife to release the juices inside. Season the fish with salt and spread a layer of butter on each one. Lay each fillet on to its own rectangle of paper.

Tuck a short frond of wild fennel underneath each piece of fish and lay another on top. (It's so pretty like this you will want to photograph it.) Add half a tablespoon of wine over each fillet and wrap up the baking parchment to make a parcel: fold the long edges over each at the top, then fold in the short ends like a present, making sure the closures are facing upwards so that the juices can't run out and escape. Bake in the oven for around 12–15 minutes for cod or salmon fillets, or 8–10 minutes for sea bass fillets, until cooked through. Remove from the oven and transfer the fish from the paper to warmed plates; pour over the sauce from the parcel and enjoy with the Lentils in Red Wine(see page 44) or some fresh peas.

Small handful of wild fennel or dill

4 cod, salmon or sea bass fillets or haddock loins (approx. 125 g/4 oz each)

Salt

25 g (1 oz) butter

2 tablespoons white wine

BACCALÀ E CECI

# Salt Cod and Chickpeas

SERVES 4

Every Friday in winter most households in Rome cook this dish as it has become a tradition following the religious belief that you should eat fish every Friday. Our friend Anna learnt this dish from her mother-in-law and in turn has taught her daughter. *Baccalà* is salted and dried cod, which has to be soaked in water for two days with four changes of water during that time. This will soften the fish and remove the salt. At this point it can be cut off the bone and into portions. It is best to taste a little piece of the fish to see if it has been soaked enough before you use it in a recipe. It should either have no salty flavour or be gently salted, but do taste before adding further seasoning. If *baccalà* is hard to find monkfish is a good alternative to use as its meaty consistency bears up to the cooking time.

50 g (2 oz) plain (all-purpose) flour for dusting

800 g (1 lb 12 oz) *baccalà* (salt cod)

3 tablespoons extra-virgin olive oil

1 white onion, finely chopped

1 garlic clove, finely chopped

1 sprig rosemary

1 bay leaf

2 sage leaves

2 x 400 g (14 oz) tins chickpeas, drained

100 ml (3$^1$/$_2$ fl oz) white wine

Salt and freshly ground black pepper

## METHOD

Put the flour into a bowl and season the fish. Coat each piece of fish in the flour, shaking off any excess, and set on to a plate. Heat half the oil in a large frying pan over a medium heat and lightly cook the fish for about 2–3 minutes each side until just pale golden. Remove from the pan. Heat the rest of the oil and gently fry the onion, garlic, rosemary, bay and sage leaves together for a few minutes making sure they don't burn. Remove the rosemary and bay leaves and stir in half of the chickpeas. Purée the rest of the chickpeas with the white wine in a food processor until soupy. Toss the chickpeas in the pan and then put the fish on top. Pour over the puréed chickpeas and cover the pan. Cook for around 15 minutes or until the fish is cooked through. Remove from the heat and serve with rice or crusty bread.

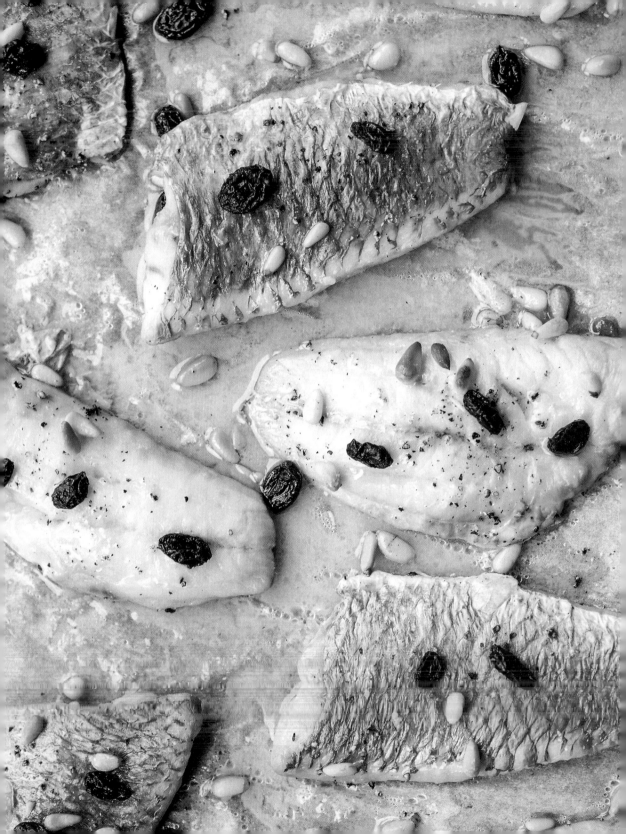

TRIGLIA CON PINOLI E UVETTA

# Red Mullet with Pine Nuts and Raisins

SERVES 4

This Roman Jewish classic is eaten at Yom Kippur and New Year. It is the most simple of recipes shown to us by Silvia Nacamulli, who teaches Italian cookery. It is surprising how impressive it is from such few ingredients, but the sweet raisins, splash of vinegar and toasted pine nuts are just lovely together. It is not traditional to use sour vinegar at New Year, which is why it is optional, but the combination of wine and vinegar is very good.

GUEST RECIPE
Silvia Nacamulli
GUEST RECIPE

METHOD

Heat the oven to 180°C (350°F/Gas 6). Lay the fillets on a baking tray (we like to line ours with baking parchment to prevent the fish sticking to the tray). Evenly scatter over the raisins, pine nuts, oil and seasoning. Bake in the oven for 15–20 minutes, depending on the size of the fish, until cooked through. Halfway through cooking, add the wine and vinegar, if using. Serve with spinach or salad.

8 red mullet fillets

2 tablespoons raisins

2 tablespoons pine nuts

3 tablespoons extra-virgin olive oil

Salt and freshly ground black pepper

3 tablespoons white wine

1 tablespoon red or white wine vinegar (optional)

ORATA IN CROSTA DI ERBE

# Sea Bream in a Herb Crust

SERVES 4

Our friend Stefania said, 'There are too many parrots singing in this cage,' when she and Giancarlo cooked together! I gazed out of the window, ignoring their banter, and studied the balconies of the flats opposite. I could see that each one had at least one terracotta pot where little chilli peppers grew next to basil, rosemary and sage. Herbs are almost never excluded from a dish here. Whether included from the start or used to finish a dish, there will be a leaf on the plate.

## METHOD

Heat the oven to 180°C (350°F/ Gas 6) and line a baking tray with baking parchment. Put the bread, garlic and herbs (torn from their stalks) into a food processor and blitz to a fine sandy texture. Pour into a bowl and mix in the cheese with a fork. Lay the fish fillets skin-side down on the lined baking tray. Sprinkle a little salt over the top of each fillet. Carefully pour the herby breadcrumbs over in a mound and finish with a drizzle of oil. Cook in the oven for around 15 minutes or until the fish is cooked through and feels firm to the touch. Serve with mashed potato, Nonna's Potatoes (see page 30) or the Roman Herb Salad (see page 32).

60 g (2 oz) soft white bread

1 garlic clove

5 large sage leaves

Small handful of mint leaves

Small handful of flat-leaf parsley leaves

Small handful of basil leaves

30 g (1 oz) Parmigiano Reggiano, finely grated

4 sea bream fillets

Salt

3 tablespoons extra-virgin olive oil

MERLUZZO COTTO SU PIETRA CON PATATE, PORCINI E POMODORI

# Cod on a Stone with Potatoes, Mushrooms and Cherry Tomatoes

SERVES 4

This bright, colourful dish is from Pierluigi restaurant in the centre of Rome. Here they use a hot stone to finish cooking the fish but you can use a frying pan. It is typical to find this at the beginning of porcini season when wooden crates of them are brought into Rome for sale. If you are lucky enough to find these use them, or swap them for chestnut mushrooms instead.

## METHOD

Heat the oven to 180°C (350°F/Gas 6). Boil the potatoes in their skins in a large saucepan of water until just tender. Depending on the size of your potatoes this could take up to 1 hour, but the flavour you achieve by using this method is worth it – leaving the skins on stops the potatoes becoming soggy. See the note at the bottom of the page if you don't have time to wait. Drain the potatoes and allow to cool. When cold, cut them into 5 mm (¼ in) thick slices. Heat 3 tablespoons of the oil in a large frying pan and fry the potato slices in batches over a medium heat until crispy and golden on both sides. Season them as you cook. Transfer to a large serving dish and keep warm in the oven.

Add a further 4 tablespoons of the oil to the pan and fry the onion and mushrooms over a medium heat for around 5 minutes until they

have softened and lightly browned. Season with salt and pepper. Meanwhile, season the cod fillets with salt and pepper and heat the remaining oil in another frying pan over a medium-high heat. Fry the cod skin-side down for around 5 minutes until the skin is crispy then flip to the other side and let the white flesh take a little colour. Gently transfer the fish to the frying pan with the onions and mushrooms, and add the tomatoes and wine. When the fish is cooked through, remove the dish of potatoes from the oven and carefully transfer the contents of the pan on top of the potatoes. Scatter over the parsley and basil. Serve with a side dish of Sautéed Spinach with Pine Nuts and Raisins on page 27 or Kale Sautéed with Garlic and Chilli on page 28.

*NB.* If you have no time, boil slices of potato or microwave them whole before slicing.

500 g (1 lb 2 oz) potatoes

9 tablespoons extra-virgin olive oil

1 large white or red onion, cut into 5mm (¼ in) slices

400 g (14 oz) fresh porcini or chestnut mushrooms, roughly sliced

4 cod fillets (approx. 150 g/5 oz each)

12 mini plum or cherry tomatoes (approx. 200 g/ 7 oz), quartered

4 tablespoons white wine

Small handful of flat-leaf parsley leaves and soft stalks, finely chopped

Small handful of basil leaves

Salt and freshly ground black pepper

# Poultry, Meat & The Fifth Quarter

The old meat market in Testaccio in Rome ran from 1890 until 1975 and employed up to 5,000 people. Complaints about the smells and the traffic it generated got it moved to a brand new site. Gleaming white metal and glass stalls means it lacks the atmosphere of its predecessor but the traders, many in their third generation of the same family, enjoy hot running water and electricity. It is held over an old Roman road and you can see below the furrows from cart wheels that are over 2,000 years old. Then, the food was brought here from the port in *amphorae*, the two handled ceramic jars. The pots were broken up and discarded, which over time built the hill called *Monte dei cocci*. It is estimated there are 53 million of them on the mound.

In this area you can see best how Romans take pleasure in eating the whole of an animal. In the local restaurants expect to see dishes such as oxtail, tripe cooked with tomato and mint, stuffed lamb's hearts, fried sweetbreads and brains. If you are lucky (depending on how you view offal) you might find *rigatoni con la pajata*, the delicacy that is milk-fed lamb's intestines with pasta.

If you are here to buy meat from the traders they will advise you how to cook foods and offer you herbs to go with it. The market is not limited to meat and is well worth a tour to taste cakes and biscuits, and admire the variety of local vegetables. Look out for red and yellow peppers displayed together, it means the greengrocer supports Roma, one of the two Roman football teams (the other being Lazio).

ZUCCHINI RIPIENI

# Stuffed Courgettes

SERVES 4

Butchers' shops are worth a visit in Rome even if you aren't intending to cook on your visit. Much imagination goes into the preparation of meat and poultry for people to take home and cook. All kinds of stuffings, wraps and herbs are used, such as guinea fowl in clay, herb-stuffed *poussins*, mushrooms stuffed with meat, and these deep green batons of hollowed-out courgettes (zucchinis). Try the butchers in Campo dei Fiori, adjacent to Il Forno bakery, and look out for Angelo Feroci in Via della Maddalena where well-dressed Romans shop for tidbits from a huge *Carrara* marble counter. Here we have given the recipe for meat-stuffed courgettes, but also an aubergine (eggplant) and walnut filling to keep on the green side. You may find you have too much filling but simply shape the rest into little patties and fry alongside the courgettes. We like to fry the courgette cores with the stuffed ones so as not to throw anything away.

FOR THE BEEF STUFFING

Mix the ingredients together in a large bowl by hand until well blended.

FOR THE AUBERGINE AND WALNUT STUFFING

Heat the oven to 180°C (350°F/Gas 6) and line a baking tray with baking parchment. Lay the aubergine discs on to the tray and brush with the oil. Season and bake for around 15–20 minutes until soft and lightly browned. Put the walnuts on to another tray and toast them in the oven with the aubergines for 8–10 minutes until just browned, then transfer to a plate to cool. Remove the aubergines from the oven and allow to cool. Use a sharp knife to finely chop the aubergines, walnuts and garlic together by hand, then combine well with the chopped nutmeg and egg in a bowl. Alternatively, use a food processor to mince the aubergine and walnuts with the rest of the ingredients. Season generously.

Prepare the courgettes by cutting each one into halves or thirds giving you approximately 8 cm (3 in) lengths and, using an apple corer, push the centres out of them. To stuff the courgettes, press a little of the filling into each of the hollows so that it is tightly packed inside. Heat the pork fat or oil in a large lidded frying pan and fry the courgettes over a medium heat (don't put the lid on yet), turning regularly, until lightly browned all around.

Add the onion, and the courgette cores if using, to the pan with the butter and cook for around 5 minutes until softened. Add the tomatoes, stir through and bring to the boil. Season to taste and put the lid on the pan. Reduce the heat and allow to simmer for around 30 minutes or until the courgettes are tender. Serve on their own, with brown rice or buttery mashed potato.

4 medium courgettes (zucchinis), (approx. 1 kg/ 2 lb 3 oz – try to find the straightest ones you can)

1 tablespoon pork fat (see page 15) or 2 tablespoons olive oil

1 red or white onion, finely chopped

25 g (1 oz) butter

1 x 400 g (14 oz) tin plum tomatoes, squashed with your hands to break them up

Salt and freshly ground black pepper

**FOR THE BEEF STUFFING**

200 g (7 oz) fine minced (ground) beef

25 g (1 oz) Parmesan, finely grated

10 g (1/2 oz) flat-leaf parsley

25 g (1 oz) breadcrumbs

1 garlic clove, finely chopped

1 egg

Salt and freshly ground black pepper

**FOR THE AUBERGINE AND WALNUT STUFFING**

1 aubergine (eggplant), cut into 1 cm (1/2 in) discs

2 tablespoons extra-virgin olive oil

50 g (2 oz) walnuts

1 garlic clove

50 g (2 oz) Parmesan, finely grated

1/2 teaspoon ground nutmeg

1 egg

Salt and freshly ground black pepper

PORCHETTA

# *Slow-roast Pork Belly with Rosemary, Sage and Garlic*

SERVES 8–10

*Porchetta*, pronounced 'porketta', is usually a whole young pig slow-roasted with golden crackling and stuffed with herbs. At home it is easy to produce a similar result with a large pork belly. We had *porchetta*, a Lazio speciality, at Osteria L'Aricciarola, one of the restaurants that specialise in this particular dish in Ariccia, just outside Rome. Every restaurant serves their own version of roast pork with a vast array of side dishes. This is rustic dining at its best: checked tablecloths, huge wooden platters of salumi and cheeses, wine from the barrel and sides served in terracotta dishes. Do venture to Ariccia if you have a chance; wander through the Sunday flea market or visit Villa d'Este and go for lunch in Ariccia afterwards – it takes a drive to get there, but there is nowhere like it. In summer, Romans escape the summer heat to sit outside, catching the cool breeze under the arched bridge that spans the town. In winter, you sit inside the restaurants alongside noisy Romans chatting and arguing over lunch.

The quality of the pork is really important for this dish – you want to find a belly of pork with plenty of fat on it. Our favourite is called Blythburgh pork from Suffolk, as the pigs are old enough to have developed a good layer of fat by the time they are slaughtered. This helps to baste the pork with fat through the cooking, so that is doesn't end up dry. Remember, 'seasoning is everything' as Giancarlo says. This is great for a dinner party served hot or cold, for a picnic or summer buffet.

2 kg (4 lb 6 oz) best-quality pork belly, skin, bored and scored

**FOR THE STUFFING**

40 g (1$^1$/$_2$ oz) sage leaves

40 g (1$^1$/$_2$ oz) rosemary sprigs

3 fat garlic cloves

2 teaspoons fine salt

1 teaspoon freshly ground black pepper

**TO COAT THE PORK**

2 tablespoons extra-virgin olive oil

1 fat garlic clove, finely chopped

2 teaspoons fine salt

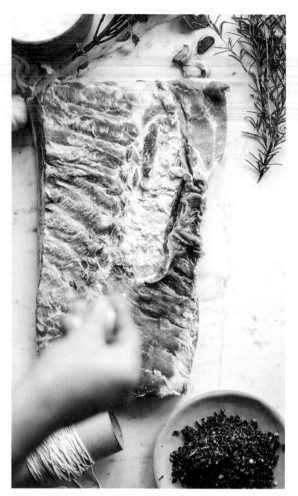 

### METHOD

Heat the oven to 160°C (320°F/Gas 4). Prepare the stuffing first. Pull the leaves from the herbs and discard the stems. Pile them on to a chopping board with the rest of the stuffing ingredients and finely chop them together with a large cook's knife. Set aside.

Lay the belly skin side up on an oven tray. Pour over a kettleful of just boiled water. The skin will swell and whiten. Pat it dry.

Lay the pork belly flat, skin-side down, on to a work surface and rub 1 tablespoon of the oil into the surface. Scatter over the chopped garlic and rub in well. Now spoon over the stuffing mixture and spread evenly over the surface. Roll up the pork belly lengthways and tie with string to secure the roll.

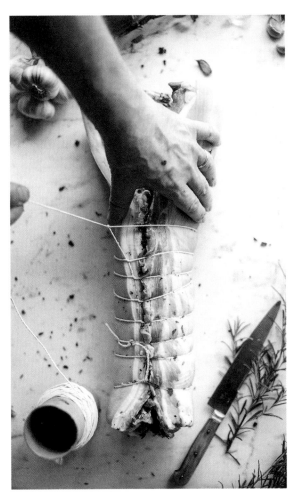

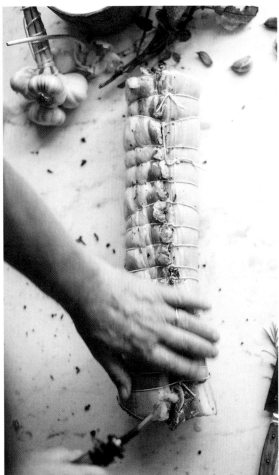

Rub the surface with the remaining oil and the salt. Lay the pork into a roasting tray and cover with foil. Roast in the oven for 3 hours. After this time, push a sharp knife into the meat; if it goes through like butter it is ready, but if there is some resistance put the pork back in for another 20 minutes before testing again. If necessary, put back in the oven and test again after another 10 minutes until the pork is done. Remove the foil, turn up the oven to 200°C (400°F/Gas 7) and cook until the skin has become crisp and golden crackling. This should take between 20–30 minutes but keep an eye on it as it burns easily. Allow the *porchetta* to rest, loosely covered with foil for 20–30 minutes, then serve with Slow-Cooked Borlotti Beans on page 35, Farro Salad on page 33 the Roman Herb Salad on page 32 and crusty bread.

WARM FARRO SALAD WITH
BACON, LEEKS & SPINACH,
PAGE 33

SLOW-COOKED
BORLOTTI BEANS WITH
TOMATOES, PAGE 35

SLOW-ROAST PORK
BELLY WITH ROSEMARY &
SAGE, PAGES 167–69

FARAONA O POLLO ALLA CACCIATORA

# Guinea Fowl or Chicken with Rosemary and Vinegar

SERVES 6

'Cacciatora' means 'hunter's wife', and in times past she would have had to rustle up a bubbling hot-pot from anything her hunter hubby dragged home from a hunt. Over the years it became an expression for a stew of mixed meats, usually cooked with tomatoes, wine and herbs. In Rome, however, 'alla cacciatora' implies meat stewed with rosemary, vinegar and anchovies, with not one tomato in sight. This dish probably dates all the way back to ancient Rome when tomatoes had not been brought ashore from South America and often foods were flavoured with herbs, vinegar and a dash of garum, the pungent anchovy sauce. The hunter's catch could be rabbit, chicken, lamb, guinea fowl (which is our favourite as it has so much flavour) or even a meaty fish such as swordfish or monkfish. The meat becomes tender with the cooking time and the juices render down to a more of a strong savoury dressing rather than a sauce. Encourage your guests to use their fingers to gnaw at the bones and give them bread to wipe up their plates.

## METHOD

Season the chicken pieces generously all over with salt and pepper. Heat the pork fat or oil in the biggest lidded frying pan you have (or use 2 if you can't fit all the chicken comfortably into 1 pan) and add the garlic and rosemary. Fry for 2–3 minutes over a medium heat until you can smell the herbs strongly; this will flavour the oil. Remove the herbs from the pan before they have a chance to burn and set aside for later. Fry the chicken pieces on all sides for about 10 minutes, browning all over, until they are a rich golden colour. Be patient and don't turn them too often; let them brown on one side and then turn to the other.

Pour in the vinegar and wine and bring to the boil. Allow the liquid to reduce for a few minutes, then add the anchovies and stir through. Put the lid on the pan and reduce the heat to a gentle simmer. Cook for 1 hour or until the meat falls easily from the bone. This will depend on your type of meat so allow enough time for it to get really soft. Check the pan every so often and add a little hot water if it looks dry. Adjust the seasoning as necessary and serve on soft polenta, Olive Mash (see page 29) or with Potato Gnocchi (see page 130) with a side of simply blanched spinach.

1.2 kg (2 lb 10 oz) chicken, jointed into 8 pieces

Salt and freshly ground black pepper

3 tablespoons rendered pork fat (see page 15) or 3 tablespoons extra virgin olive oil

2 garlic cloves, unpeeled and lightly crushed

2 x 15 cm (6 in) sprigs rosemary

4 tablespoons white wine vinegar

100 ml (3$^1$/$_2$ fl oz) white wine

4 tinned anchovy fillets (if salted rinse well, if in oil don't)

ABBACCHIO ALLA CACCIATORA

# Slow-cooked Lamb with Garlic, Anchovies and Rosemary

SERVES 6–8

Traditionally this is made with a milk-fed lamb between 20 days and 1 month old. This ensures soft and tender meat. However, as milk-fed lamb is difficult to get hold of unless you own your own livestock, we follow the same flavours but use a shoulder of lamb, or cheaper cuts like knuckle and shank. I like to do this for a lunch and serve it with the Salt-Baked Onions on page 38 and Nonna's Potatoes on page 30. With a good bottle of red wine it feels like a proper Roman feast. Italians enjoy the juices from the pan rather than a gravy but we've written a recipe for one as half of our family are English and like our gravy! Any leftover cooked lamb can be used to make meatballs; just follow the recipe for the *Polpette di Bollito* on page 90 substituting lamb for the beef.

1 medium shoulder of lamb (around 2 kg / 4 lb 6 oz)

2 sprigs rosemary (approx. 20 cm / 8 in long)

40 g (1½ oz) anchovy fillets in oil

2 fat garlic cloves

Salt

3 celery sticks, halved widthways

2 carrots, halved lengthways

200 ml (7 fl oz) white or red wine vinegar

200 ml (7 fl oz) water

**FOR THE GRAVY**

100 ml (3½ fl oz) red wine

300–500 ml (10–17 fl oz) hot water

25 g (1 oz) butter

20 g (¾ oz) '00' or plain (all-purpose) flour

Salt and freshly ground black pepper

### METHOD

Allow the lamb to come to room temperature; this should take around 30 minutes and will ensure the lamb cooks evenly. Cut away any really tough skin from the top; waxy fat is good so you can leave that. Heat the oven to 220°C (430°F/Gas 9).

Pull the leaves off the rosemary and discard the stem. Put the anchovies, garlic and rosemary together on a board and chop together until you have a rough paste. Use a sharp knife to make around 20 incisions in the lamb and push a pinch of the paste into each small cut. Lay the celery and carrots into the centre of a roasting tray to form a trivet for the lamb to sit on; this will keep it out of the water and vinegar in the dish. Rub the lamb all over with salt and place it on top of the vegetables. Pour the vinegar and water into the tray. Wrap the tray tightly in 2 layers of foil and bake in the oven for 10 minutes. Turn the oven down to 170°C (340°F/Gas 5) and roast for another 3 hours. After this time, remove the foil (carefully as the steam rushes out) and pull the shoulder bone away slightly. The meat around it should give easily, be tender and about to fall off the

bone. If it is not done to your liking replace the foil and put the lamb back into the oven (this can happen if the shoulder is large). Remove the lamb from the roasting tray and set aside on a plate to rest covered in foil and a cloth.

To make the gravy, strain the juices from the cooking pan into a medium saucepan through a fine sieve. Let the juices settle and scoop off the fat from the surface with a ladle and discard. Add the red wine and hot water to the juices and stir through – how much water you will need to add depends on how much liquid you already have from the lamb juices and how much gravy you want to make. Thicken the sauce by mixing the butter and flour together in a separate small saucepan over a gentle heat. Whisk a little of this mixture, the roux, into the gravy and cook over a medium heat until thickened. If it doesn't get thick enough after a few minutes, add a little more roux. Season to taste and pour into a warm gravy boat or jug. Put the lamb into a warm serving dish with the gravy on the side. Serve with Salt-Baked Onions (see page 38), Nonna's Potatoes (see page 30) or Potato Gnocchi (see page 130).

POLLO ALLA ROMANA

# *Roman Chicken with Peppers*

SERVES 4

First choose your football team! If it is Roma you will delight in cooking red and yellow (bell) peppers in your team colours. If it's Lazio you might omit the peppers altogether or only use red. For a faster version of this dish the peppers can be put in pieces halfway through cooking, but my favourite version of this dish was at Dar Moschino in Garbatella where the peppers were blackened first and peeled.

If you have time to take a tour out of town and you want to try the real thing as far as Roman cooking is concerned, do take a ride to Dar Moschino. It used to be a wine and oil shop until they started up a small kitchen. The wine prices are still exceptionally low, so that might make up the cost of a taxi there and back. Don't expect English to be spoken or insincere smiles, but expect to taste the best traditional Roman cooking.

## METHOD

Prepare the peppers as you would for the *Peperonata* on page 73. Cut or tear each one, once peeled, into 10 long strips and set aside. Break up the tomatoes using a sharp knife while they are in the tin or tip them into a bowl and squeeze them with your hands.

Season the chicken generously on all sides. Fry the chicken in the oil in a large non-stick frying pan over a medium heat for about 10 minutes until it's a rich golden brown. Tip away most of the excess fat leaving just a couple of tablespoons in the pan. Add the garlic, capers and oregano, and fry for 2 minutes over a low heat so that the garlic doesn't brown at all. Pour in the white wine, increase the heat to medium, and allow it to reduce for a couple of minutes. Add the peppers and tomatoes and stir to combine them with the chicken pieces. Bring to the boil, then reduce the heat to simmer gently over a medium–low heat, uncovered, for around 30 minutes, or until the chicken is cooked through and comes away easily from the bone. Move the pieces around occasionally to make sure they are covered in the sauce and are cooked evenly. When the chicken is done, taste the sauce and adjust the seasoning as necessary. Serve with Nonna's Potatoes (see page 30), polenta, brown rice or either of the spinach dishes on pages 27–28.

3 (bell) peppers (red or a mixture of red and yellow)

1 x 400 g (14 oz) tin whole plum tomatoes

800 g (1 lb 12 oz) chicken (either 1 chicken jointed into pieces or all thighs)

2 tablespoons sunflower oil

2 garlic cloves, finely chopped

1 tablespoon capers

1 teaspoon dried oregano

100 ml (3½ fl oz) white wine

Salt and freshly ground black pepper

ANIMELLE ALLA GRIGLIA CON PURÈ DI PATATE ALLE OLIVE

# Grilled Sweetbreads on Olive Mash

SERVES 4

Sweetbreads are hugely popular in Rome as, among other offal, they made up part of the wages for the butchers at the slaughterhouse. They were either eaten at home or sold to restaurants. Delicate in flavour, sweetbreads are delicious if you are prepared to try them. We had them at the elegant Al Ceppo restaurant in Parioli where they were served on top of yellow potato Olive Mash (see page 29) and thyme collected that morning from owner Maria Cristina's terrace.

### METHOD

Using a sharp knife, remove the outer membrane from the sweetbreads. Bring the water and vinegar to the boil in a medium saucepan and drop in the sweetbreads. Cook for 8 minutes or until cooked through. Drain and allow to cool. Cut into bite-size pieces and season well with salt and pepper. Heat the oil in a small frying pan and fry the sweetbreads over a medium heat for a couple of minutes until lightly browned. Turn them a couple of times to ensure even cooking. Remove from the pan and serve straight away with the Olive Mash (see page 29).

400 g (14 oz) veal sweetbreads

1.5 litres (51 fl oz) water

3 tablespoons white wine vinegar

2 tablespoons extra-virgin olive oil

Salt and freshly ground black pepper

1 quantity Olive Mash (see page 29)

CODA ALLA VACCINARA

# *Oxtail Stew*

SERVES 6

Beef stew in all its forms is essential to the average Roman kitchen. It gives nourishment, comfort and that sense of security that comes from a ritual that you perform so regularly you can't imagine life without it. Even *ragu*, or meat sauce, that is made all over Italy is a form of stewed beef. Whether the meat is whole or ground, that marriage of beef and tomatoes cooked for a very long time together is hard to beat.

In Rome the Jewish have 'stracotto' meaning 'overcooked', born from a time when only the cheaper cuts were available to them. It was traditionally cooked on the ashes of a fire on a Friday so that it was still warm on the Sabbath when cooking was prohibited. Out of the many beef stew recipes, we have chosen to include *Garofolato di Manzo* (see page 198) made with a whole piece of meat pierced with spices, and *Coda alla Vaccinara*, which uses oxtail. It is a good idea to make this dish a day before you want to eat, allowing the fat to come to the surface overnight so that it can be removed.

1.2 kg (2 lb 10 oz) oxtail

2 tablespoons
sunflower oil

200 ml (7 oz)
white wine

2 x 400 g (14 oz)
tins plum tomatoes

1 heaped tablespoon
tomato purée (paste)

1 small cinnamon stick

500 ml (17 fl oz) homemade
meat or vegetable stock,
as necessary (see page 107)

FOR THE *SOFFRITTO*

6 celery sticks with leaves,
coarsely chopped into
5 mm (1/4 in) cubes

2 medium white onions,
coarsely chopped

2 carrots,
coarsely chopped

8 tablespoons
extra-virgin olive oil

3 teaspoons fine salt

1/2 teaspoon freshly
ground black pepper

3 bay leaves

## METHOD

Fill a large saucepan three quarters full with water and bring to the boil. Add the oxtail and bring the water back to the boil, then remove the oxtail from the water. Pour the water and any scum away. Boiling the oxtail like this will clean it and get rid of some of the fat.

Make the *soffritto* in a large saucepan; fry the vegetables in the olive oil with the seasoning and bay leaves for around 5–10 minutes over a medium heat until tender.

Heat the sunflower oil in a large frying pan over a medium–high heat and brown the oxtail all over. Transfer the oxtail to the *soffritto* and then pour over the wine. Allow it to reduce for a few minutes. Add the tomatoes, tomato purée and cinnamon. Wash the tomato tins out with a little water and add this to the tomatoes. Add enough stock to cover the oxtails. Turn down to simmer and cook, covered, for 5 hours or until the meat falls from the bones. During cooking, turn the oxtails to make sure they don't stick and top up with a little stock, if necessary, so that they are always covered. You can also cook this in the oven: heat the oven to 160°C (320°F/Gas 4) and cook the stew in a casserole dish. Serve with mashed potato or Potato Gnocchi (see page 130).

OSSO BUCO ALLA ROMANA

# *Roman-style Osso Buco*

SERVES 6

*Osso buco*, meaning bone with a hole, is usually linked with Milan where it is served with risotto. However, Rome also claims it as its own, and here it is served with mashed potato or potato gnocchi. We loved it at Gino, a buzzing trattoria crammed with Romans. Maria Cristina at restaurant Al Ceppo told us that her secret was to put a couple of anchovies in the sauce.

### METHOD

Heat the oven to 180°C (350°F/Gas 6). First prepare the carrots, celery and onion for the *soffritto* by either chopping them finely by hand or by whizzing them in a food processor.

Use a pair of scissors to snip around the fatty edges of the *osso buco*. This will help them stay in shape rather than split their sides. Season each one with salt and pepper, and then lightly coat them with flour. Tap off the excess.

Put all of the *soffritto* ingredients into the olive oil in a large ovenproof frying pan or casserole dish over a medium heat and fry for around 10 minutes until the vegetables are softened and have lost their colour.

Heat the sunflower oil in a second frying pan and, when hot, fry the *osso buco* over a medium heat for around 10 minutes until golden on both sides. Remove them from the pan and add to the *soffritto*. Add the wine and allow to reduce for 2 minutes before adding the tomato purée and stock. Transfer the pan or casserole dish to the oven and cook, uncovered, for about 1–1½ hours until the *osso buco* is soft and falls easily from the bone.

6 *ossi buchi* or 1 leg of veal cut into 6

Salt and freshly ground black pepper

50 g (2 oz) plain (all-purpose) flour for coating

100 ml (3½ fl oz) sunflower oil

600 ml (20 fl oz) dry white wine

2 tablespoons tomato purée (paste)

150 ml (5 fl oz) homemade meat or vegetable stock (see page 107)

#### FOR THE *SOFFRITTO*

2–3 large carrots (approx. 200 g/7 oz)

4–6 celery sticks (approx. 250 g/9 oz)

200 g (7 oz) onions

100 ml (3½ oz) olive oil

2 bay leaves

2 tinned anchovy fillets

2 garlic cloves

2 sprigs rosemary

POLLO ALL'INSALATA NEL GIARDINO DELL ERBE

# Chicken in the Herb Garden

SERVES 8

This eccentric and beautiful dish is from our expert guide to hidden Rome and friend Ginevra Lovatelli; she was shown it by her friend Lorenzo who likes to make it in summer and serves it on a large platter with cheeses and other salads. It is made with seven different herbs, hence the name. The chicken is beautifully soft as it is poached in vinegar, which you would think makes it very acidic but actually the flavour mellows with the marinating and the addition of a good olive oil. It can be made from a variety of vinegars – the best are wine, balsamic or cider – and a wide variety of herbs. Ginevra guides people around the sights of Rome discussing the art work as well as the architecture of the eternal city. Having now studied ancient Roman recipes we think this recipe could be as old as the Parthenon.

## METHOD

Cut each chicken breast lengthways into 8 long strips so you have 32 strips altogether. Lay the strips between 2 pieces of baking parchment and gently bash them out with a rolling pin to make long strips around 5 mm (¼ in) thick. Season each piece with salt and pepper. Roll the chicken strips up into spirals and secure with toothpicks. Bring the vinegar, water and a pinch of salt to the boil in a large saucepan and then add the chicken. Reduce the heat and simmer for around 15–20 minutes until the chicken is cooked through.

Drain the chicken and discard the liquid. The chicken might appear speckled in appearance but don't worry about it. Remove the toothpicks, cut the chicken into slices about 1 cm (½ in) thick and put the spirals on a large plate. Season, drizzle over the oil and scatter over the herbs. Leave to marinate loosely covered in baking parchment in the fridge for 24 hours. If you are in a real hurry it is also good after a couple of hours, but the flavour improves with time. Bring to room temperature before eating and serve with salad and crusty bread.

4 chicken breasts
(approx. 800 g/1 lb 12 oz)

600 ml (20 fl oz) wine,
cider or balsamic vinegar

400 ml (13 fl oz) water

Salt

6 tablespoons single
estate extra-virgin
olive oil

40 g (1¹/₂ oz) mixed
fresh herbs, such as
tarragon, basil, mint,
parsley, sage, thyme,
rosemary, finely chopped

Salt and freshly
ground black pepper

SCALOPPINE DI VITELLO CON MARSALA E ARANCIA

# *Escalope of veal with Marsala and Orange*

SERVES 4

Our Roman friend Stefania has three in her family and most evenings she makes a simple supper for her trio with only a few ingredients on the plate. Mainly she uses only three flavours as she doesn't like to overpower the main ingredient; she feels that should be allowed to shine through. When we worked together at her house she realised she had a whole repertoire of family recipes that each had only three main ingredients!

GUEST RECIPE
Stefania
Menichetti
GUEST RECIPE

**METHOD**

Season and lightly flour the escalopes. Heat the oil in a large frying pan over a medium–high heat and add the escalopes. Fry for about 1–2 minutes until lightly golden on one side, then turn over and fry for another 2 minutes until golden on both sides. Add the strip of orange peel and the marsala, and allow to reduce for a couple of minutes. Pour in the orange juice and water, then add the butter, and swirl through with the juices in the pan to form the sauce. Serve straight away with mashed potato or Nonna's Potatoes (see page 30) and Sautéed Spinach or Kale (see page 27 or 28).

6 veal or turkey escalopes

Plain (all-purpose) flour, for dusting

3 tablespoons extra-virgin olive oil

1 x 8 cm (3 in) strip orange peel

60 ml (2 fl oz) marsala or sweet wine

2 tablespoons orange juice

3 tablespoons water

30 g (1 oz) butter

Salt and freshly ground black pepper

STRACCETTI E RUCOLA

# Beef Strips or 'Rags' with Rocket

SERVES 4

Italian butchers are used to people asking for the beef cut called *strachetti*, meaning 'rags', which are very thinly cut pieces of raw meat. It is often done on a slicer but most butchers outside Italy will only cut cooked beef on a slicer. Ask for rump steak as thinly cut as they can with their ultra-sharp butchers' knives. If the slices are more than half a centimetre thick, put them between two sheets of baking parchment and bash them out with the base of a small saucepan or a meat mallet. This will tenderise the beef and make it cook quickly.

6 tablespoons extra-virgin olive oil

250 g (8$^1$/$_2$ fl oz) porcini or chestnut mushrooms, finely sliced

1 garlic clove, peeled and lightly crushed

1 sprig rosemary

$^1$/$_2$ teaspoon salt, plus extra for seasoning

$^1$/$_2$ teaspoon freshly ground black pepper, plus extra for seasoning

500 g (1 lb 2 oz) rump steak, cut into 5 mm ($^1$/$_4$ in) thick slices

Good handful of rocket (arugula) leaves

2 teaspoons aged balsamic vinegar

Best-quality extra-virgin olive oil, to serve

METHOD

Heat 4 tablespoons of the oil in a large frying pan. Fry the mushrooms over a high heat with the garlic and rosemary, and add the salt and pepper.

When the mushrooms are lightly browned, remove from the pan and keep them warm in a heatproof dish in a low oven. Discard the garlic and rosemary and wipe the pan with kitchen paper to remove any bits and oil still in it.

Season the steak pieces and heat the remaining oil in the frying pan over a high heat. When hot, fry the steak for 1–2 minutes, turning them over once during cooking – you may need to do this in batches so you can fry the slices in a single layer in the pan. When just cooked through, remove from the heat and put the steak into a warm serving dish.

Scatter the mushrooms and rocket on top and drizzle with the balsamic vinegar and a swirl of your best olive oil. Serve straight away.

SALTIMBOCCA ALLA ROMANA

# *Escalopes with Prosciutto and Sage Leaves in a Wine and Butter Sauce*

SERVES 6

Just the title makes my mouth water. *Saltimbocca* means literally 'jump in the mouth', maybe because it usually has this effect on people! This is traditionally made with veal, but we often use chicken instead. Chicken meat is not as strong as veal, so it has to be 'bashed out' with a little more care but the result is tender, economical and more easily accessible than veal. This is our friend Wendy Holloway's favourite dish to teach on her Roman cookery courses as it is quick, effective and popular with her guests.

## METHOD

Lay each escalope between 2 sheets of baking parchment and use a meat mallet or the base of a small saucepan to bash them out to approximately 5 mm (¼ in) thick. Remove the baking parchment, lay the escalopes on a large plate and place a slice of prosciutto over each escalope. Use a toothpick to then secure a sage leaf over the top of each one. Press them down lightly to secure the escalope and ham together. Cover with baking parchment and put in the fridge for about 10 minutes or up to 1 day, until you are ready to cook.

Take the escalopes from the fridge and remove the baking parchment. Put an ovenproof serving dish in a low oven to warm. Put some flour in a shallow bowl and lightly coat each escalope in flour, shaking off the excess. Heat the oil in a large non-stick frying pan over a medium heat and fry the escalopes, prosciutto-side down first, for about 2–3 minutes until golden; turn over and fry for another 2–3 minutes until golden and cooked through. Transfer the escalopes to the warmed serving dish.

Drain the oil from the pan, add the wine and butter and reduce for a couple of minutes. Serve this buttery sauce with the escalopes and either of the spinach recipes on pages 27–28, Olive Mash on page 29 or Nonna's Potatoes on page 30.

6 veal or chicken escalopes

6 slices prosciutto

6 large sage leaves

Salt and freshly ground black pepper

'00' or plain (all-purpose) flour for coating

4 tablespoons extra-virgin olive oil

125 ml (4 fl oz) dry white wine

25 g (1 oz) butter

GAROFOLATO DI MANZO

# Beef Casserole with Red Wine and Cloves

SERVES 6–8

The Italian name for this dish comes from its use of cloves known as *chiodi di garofano*, which translates as 'nails of carnation', and carnations can also be known as 'clove pinks', so linguistically there is some link there! Cloves were found burnt into the floor of a kitchen dated 1700 BC in Syria, and Roman writer Pliny the Elder wrote about them in the 1st century AD, so they certainly have been in use in Italy for centuries.

Pork fat is cut and chopped with the herbs to make a herb paste; this is a typical old Italian way to start a sauce that results in a wonderful depth of flavour. Often butchers will give (or sell you cheaply) pieces of leftover pork fat, which can be rendered down and used in place of oil or butter. It is very useful in Roman dishes.

This casserole can be served in slices, reheated in the sauce, or the sauce can be used as a pasta sauce. Our butchers Aubrey Allen recommended using a leg of mutton or lean beef rump, as both are lean but can withstand the long cooking time. In Rome they use a cut called *girello* from the back of the thigh, which is similar to our topside.

1.5 kg (3 lb 5 oz) beef (thick flank, topside or leg of mutton cut)

Salt and freshly ground black pepper

50 g (2 oz) pork fat or fatty streaky unsmoked bacon, cut into 1 cm (1/2 in) strips

50 g (2 oz) salted butter

2 garlic cloves, peeled and lightly crushed

300 ml (10 fl oz) red wine

5 cloves

1 onion, finely chopped

2 medium carrots, finely chopped

2 celery sticks, finely chopped

4 tablespoons olive oil

2 tablespoons tomato purée (paste)

200 ml (7 fl oz) hot water

**FOR THE HERB PASTE**

50 g (2 oz) pork fat or unsmoked fatty streaky bacon

3 cloves, crushed in a pestle and mortar

1 fat garlic clove, peeled

1 teaspoon salt

1/2 teaspoon freshly ground black pepper

2 teaspoons dried marjoram or oregano

2 teaspoons thyme leaves

## METHOD

Preheat the oven to 170°C (340°F/Gas 5). First make the herb paste; put the pork fat on to a chopping board with the rest of the herb paste ingredients and chop together until you have formed a thick herby paste. Make around 15 small incisions in the meat, around 3 cm (1 in) deep, with a sharp knife and use your finger to push in about 1 teaspoon of the paste into each hole until it is all used up. Roll the meat into a neat shape and tie securely with string. Season with salt and pepper.

Heat the pork fat or bacon with the butter in a large high-sided lidded frying pan or a casserole dish over a medium heat. Add the garlic and sauté for 2 minutes,

then remove before it burns and set aside. Add the meat to the pan and brown all over, then add the wine and cloves and cook for 5–10 minutes.

In a separate frying pan, fry the chopped vegetables in the oil over a medium heat for about 7 minutes until softened. Mix the tomato purée with the hot water in a jug and add this to the beef along with the softened vegetables and reserved garlic. Cover the pan and simmer gently for 2 1/2 hours until the meat is tender. Remove from the heat and allow to rest for 20 minutes before slicing and serving with the sauce.

# *Dolci*

What Rome lacks in indigenous desserts it makes up for in *gelato*, which has its own chapter in this book (see page 231). However, creamy cool ricotta, the by-product of making mozzarella and pecorino, makes a regular appearance. Ancient Romans used honey to sweeten it to make desserts. In his work *De Agricultura* Cato the Censor, otherwise known as Cato the Elder, writes of a recipe for *savillum*, a sheep's milk ricotta cheesecake with honey, egg and flour. It was centuries later when the use of ricotta sweetened with sugar and flavoured with *cedro*, or citron, came to Rome from Sicily with the Jews.

Biscuits are one of Rome's sweet pleasures. Visit any patisserie and you will see a selection of biscuits ready to be packaged up in cellophane and ribbons, and taken as gifts when you are asked to lunch or dinner. Pretty cherry jam tarts decorated with crosses sit next to cinnamon biscotti, coconut kisses and dark pink *biscotti di vino* (red wine biscuits). *Pan giallo,* a fruit and nut cake, and *mostaccioli*, chocolate glazed biscuits, are spiced Christmas treats that have been made since famous Rennaissance chef Bartolomeo Scappi's days in the 1500s. When nuts are used they are generally Lazio-grown hazelnuts or almonds from the south of Italy.

We have included tiramisu, which might of course make a few people groan with 'Oh no, not again', however a trip to Pompi, the so-called home of tiramisu in Rome, and the fact that so many of our friends in Rome make it regularly, awakened our imagination, so here we include one classic (child friendly without the alcohol) and two wickedly adult versions for those days when cautions are thrown to the wind.

BARCHETTA DI MELONE

# *Melon Boats*

Fresh fruit stands are found all over Rome offering enticing cut fruit and smoothies made with the local water. I saw this way of serving them out of the corner of my eye as we flashed past a stand in a taxi on a warm summer night. Luminous displays of fruits glowed from the kiosk and an inventive seller had made up these bright stripy boats from alternating varieties of melon.

TORTA BIANCA

# *White Ginger Cheesecake*

SERVES 8

This is to me the most perfect cheesecake. It has depth, but is not cloying; it is light but flavourful, and it seems a hit with everyone who tries it. This is a recipe from Maestro Martino who was a 15th-century chef who wrote *Libro de Arte Coquinaria*, 'The Art of Cooking'. It was later translated into Latin by Platina, his co-author, who described him as the 'prince of cooks'. White foods such as this were a luxury and seen as rare and pure. Martino used a white fresh cheese and to imitate this we have use a mixture of ricotta and cream cheese to achieve the necessary texture and tang. For the ginger, he asks for 'the whitest ginger', which would have been powdered or at least firm enough in root form to chop finely or grate. We like the flavour of fresh ginger now that it is readily available. To finish, the tart was sprinkled with rosewater and more sugar, but I prefer to leave it pure and simple.

It may seem mad to use unsalted butter and then add salt, but I have made grave mistakes before when butter has been saltier than I imagined and so I prefer to buy unsalted and add my own pinch of salt to taste. I suspect this tart was inspired by the Jewish combination of ricotta and sugar, which was probably brought to Rome from Sicily by the Jews in the fifteenth century.

### FOR THE PASTRY

125 g (4 oz) unsalted butter, softened

250 g (9 oz/2 cups) '00' or plain (all-purpose) flour

Pinch of salt

50 g (2 oz/$^1/_4$ cup) caster (superfine) sugar

2 tablespoons cold water

### FOR THE FILLING

250 g (9 oz) ricotta

250 g (9 oz) cream cheese

100 g (3$^1/_2$ oz/ scant $^1/_2$ cup) caster (superfine) sugar

100 g (3$^1/_2$ oz) unsalted butter, softened

Small pinch of salt, to taste

50 g (2 oz) fresh ginger, finely grated, or 4 teaspoons ground ginger

100 ml (3$^1/_2$ fl oz) milk

4 egg whites

### METHOD

Use a loose-bottomed 2 cm (¾ in) deep 24 cm (9½ in) pie tin or a shallow tin lined with a circle of baking parchment. If your tin does not have a loose bottom, put long strips of baking parchment into it in a cross to help you lift out the cheesecake when cool.

First make the pastry by combining all the ingredients briefly in a food processor. If you prefer to work by hand, rub the butter into the flour, salt and sugar between your fingers to make breadcrumbs, then add the water and form a dough. Wrap it in baking parchment and chill in the fridge for 20 minutes. Heat the oven to 180°C (350°F/Gas 6).

Roll out the pastry to around 3 mm (¼ in) thick. Line the tin with the pastry allowing the edges to flop over the sides of the tin. Bake the pastry blind (without the filling in) with a lining of baking parchment filled with baking beans or uncooked rice for 10 minutes. Remove from the oven and remove the paper and beans. Put the pastry back into the oven for a further 5 minutes until lightly golden. Remove from the oven and allow to cool. Turn the oven down to 170°C (340°F/Gas 5). Trim the excess pastry hanging over the edge of the tin with a sharp knife. Set aside.

To make the filling mix all the ingredients together, except the egg whites, with a whisk in a large bowl. With a clean whisk, whip the egg whites into stiff peaks and then gently fold them into the cheese mixture with a large metal spoon or spatula. Pour the mixture into the pastry case and put it back into the oven for 1 hour. Remove the cheesecake from the oven and allow to cool to room temperature before removing it from the tin. Serve at room temperature or chilled from the fridge.

TORTA DI MELE A 'LA CAMPANA'

# Roman Apple Cake from La Campana

SERVES 8-10

Two enormous round tins of apple cake are cooked every day in La Campana restaurant, and each day they are eaten up, so the process continues the following day. La Campana is the oldest restaurant in Rome and has been run by four generations of the same Trancassini family. This is one recipe they never take off the menu and, having eaten it, I can see why. The apples and sponge merge into one another under a layer of sticky apricot jam. Served slightly warm with a dollop of rosemary ice cream (see Herb Ice Cream, page 240), this has to be one of my favourite desserts.

200 g (7 oz / 1²/₃ cups) '00' flour (or use self-raising flour and omit the baking powder), plus 1 tablespoon for sprinkling

150 g (2 oz) caster (superfine) sugar

3 eggs

100 ml (3¹/₂ fl oz) milk

1 vanilla pod, seeds scraped or 1 teaspoon vanilla extract

1 level teaspoon ground cinnamon

Finely grated zest of ¹/₂ lemon

2 flat teaspoons baking powder

100 g (3¹/₂ oz) unsalted butter, at room temperature

3–4 apples, peeled and cut into 5 mm (¹/₄ in) thick slices

200 g (7 oz) apricot jam

## METHOD

Heat the oven to 160°C (320°F/ Gas 4). Line the bottom of a 24 cm (9½ in) cake tin with baking parchment torn into a large circle so that when pushed down it protrudes above the edge of the tin by around 4 cm (1½ in). Using a whisk, mix together the 200 g (7 oz/1²/₃ cups) flour, the sugar, eggs, milk, vanilla cinnamon, lemon zest and baking powder. Stir well to combine. Tear the butter into small chunks with your fingers and whisk them in. The pieces of butter will melt as the cake cooks, leaving holes that keep the cake moist and buttery. Pour the batter into the lined tin. Gently sprinkle the tablespoon of flour over the surface of the sponge. Place the apple slices over the top, fanning them out, starting from the outside and working in. The apples should overlap each other slightly;

use the largest slices on the outside and place the smallest slices in the middle of the tart.

Warm the jam in a small saucepan over a medium heat and add a little water if it is very thick – you want it to be just loose enough to pour but not runny. Gently spoon half the jam over the top of the apples.

Bake in the centre of the oven for 35–40 minutes until the cake is set; test it by inserting a skewer into the centre of the cake, which should come out clean when it's done. As soon as the cake comes out of the oven, brush on the rest of the jam – you may need to warm it up again slightly to get it to the right consistency. Allow the cake to cool and serve warm or with rosemary ice cream (see Herb Ice Cream, page 240).

TORTA DI PERE IN ZUPPA DI CIOCCOLATO

# Warm Pear and Orange Cake in Milk Chocolate Soup

**MAKES 12 SMALL CAKES**
**SOUP SERVES 10–12** (makes approx. 250 ml / 8½ fl oz)

This heavenly dessert recipe was based on one we ate at Al Ceppo restaurant in Parioli, Rome. Soft pear in a light sponge with crunchy hazelnut ice cream makes a perfect contrast to the intense and bittersweet chocolate sauce using only the sugar in the chocolate for sweetness.

## METHOD

Heat the oven to 180°C (350°F/Gas 6). Grease the moulds in a 12 hole muffin tin for the cakes, unless they are silicone. When the oven is hot, place the sugar on a baking tray lined with baking parchment and heat in the oven for 5 minutes.

Whisk the eggs and egg yolk in a large bowl with a hand-held blender for 1 minute. Add the warm sugar and the orange zest, then continue to whisk until the mixture forms a ribbon-like trail when the whisk is lifted. (This will take about 5 minutes, so persevere to get a really frothy and light mixture. To check you've whisked enough, turn off the blender and lift the beaters from the mix, making a circle with the beaters over the bowl; you should be able to see a line of the mixture sit on the surface before sinking in. If there is no trail, continue to whisk. When it is ready, very gently fold in the sifted flour, salt, and the cubes of pear using as few movements as possible; you don't want to lose the precious air you have whipped in. Melt the butter in a microwave or in a small saucepan and when just runny, mix in with the rest of the ingredients,

gently folding it as before. Divide the mixture between the moulds to just below the top of each one.

Transfer to the oven and bake for 15–20 minutes or until golden brown and a skewer inserted into the centre of the cakes comes out clean. Allow the cakes to cool for 10 minutes before removing from the moulds. Leave to cool on a wire rack. To serve, briefly heat the cakes for 5 minutes in an oven heated to 180°C (350°F/Gas 6). Swirl a little Milk Chocolate Soup (below) into a wide bowl, set a cake into it and then finish with a scoop of Toasted Hazelnut Ice Cream (see page 240), a few slices of pear and some tarragon leaves.

For the milk chocolate soup: Heat the milk, cream, butter and salt together in a medium saucepan over a medium-high heat. Bring to the boil, stirring frequently with a wooden spoon, and then remove from the heat. Stir in the chocolate until it is melted and smooth. Use straight away or allow to cool and reheat gently in a bowl over a simmering pan of boiling water, or briefly in the microwave.

**FOR THE CAKES**

60 g (2 oz/¼ cup) caster (superfine) sugar

2 eggs

1 egg yolk

Zest of ½ orange

60 g (2 oz/½ cup) '00' or plain (all-purpose) flour, sifted

Pinch of salt

25 g (1 oz) unsalted butter

3 pears: 1 peeled and cut into 1 cm cubes; 2 sliced, to serve

Handful of tarragon, to serve

**FOR THE MILK CHOCOLATE SOUP**

8 tablespoons whole milk

4 tablespoons double (heavy) cream

25 g (1 oz) unsalted butter

Pinch of salt

100 g (3½ oz) milk chocolate (min. 70% cocoa solids), broken into small pieces

RICOTTA MONTATA CON RUM E COMPOSTA DI BACCHE

# Whipped Ricotta with Rum and Fresh Berry Compote

SERVES 6-12

This glorious marriage of flavours has been around for centuries in Italy. It soothes with its cuddle of creamy sweetened ricotta. Add crushed Amaretti and preserved cherries; our favourite are the amarena cherries made by Fabbri and sold in pretty blue and white patterned jars. If you can't find those, raspberries and strawberries when in season are also a suitable companion.

**METHOD**

Put all of the ingredients into a bowl and whisk together by hand or with a hand-held blender until smooth. Adjust the sugar and rum to your taste. Serve chilled in either 6 wine glasses or 12 shot glasses on its own or with a few cherries and some crushed Amaretti biscuits.

350 g (12 oz) ricotta

150 g (5 oz) whipping cream

50 g (2 oz) icing (confectioners') sugar

50 ml (2 fl oz) dark rum

**TO SERVE (OPTIONAL)**

1 jar preserved cherries or other soft fruit

Handful of *Amaretti* biscuits

BISCOTTI DI SEMI DI SESAMO E MIELE

# Sesame and Honey Biscuits

MAKES 30 BISCUITS

A thousand years on and we are starting to enjoy foods again that aren't packed with sugar, hydrogenated fat and white refined flour. This recipe could come from a modern baking book today. Instead, it comes from Mark Grant's *Roman Cookery*, his cookbook of ancient Roman recipes. Both these biscuits and the Fried Ravioli Filled with Walnuts and Dates (see opposite) are delicious sticky treats from the late second century, written about in Athenaeus's description of a fictitious feast, including the gossip and debates of the guests, called The Partying Professors. The biscuits are lightly sweetened with honey, as sugar was almost only used for medicinal purposes, and have a gentle nuttiness from the spelt flour and seeds. Sesame seeds are full of beneficial omega-6 oils, vitamins and flavonoids, so this is one biscuit you needn't feel bad about eating! Buckwheat flour also works and gives a gluten-free result. See photo overleaf.

100 g (3$^1$/$_2$ oz) sesame seeds

60 g (2 oz / $^1$/$_2$ cup) spelt or buckwheat flour

1 tablespoon extra-virgin olive oil

2 tablespoons mild honey

3 tablespoons water

1 teaspoon vanilla extract or seeds from 1 vanilla pod

## METHOD

Toast the sesame seeds in a dry frying pan, tossing frequently to stop them burning, for a few minutes over a medium heat until golden. Pour them on to a plate and when cool, combine the seeds with the rest of the ingredients in a bowl and bring everything together into a slightly wet pastry dough. Rest the pastry in a covered bowl in the fridge for 1 hour, where the seeds and flour will soak up the liquid.

Heat the oven to 180°C (350°F/ Gas 6) and line a baking tray with baking parchment. Lightly flour your work surface and roll out the pastry to around 5 mm (¼ in) thick. Cut the biscuits into rounds using a 5 cm (2 in) cutter or an upturned wine glass. Place them on to the baking tray and bake for 5–10 minutes until lightly browned. Cool on a wire rack and serve with sweet wine, coffee, any of the ice creams on page 240 or with the Whipped Ricotta with Rum (see page 213).

RAVIOLI FRITTI RIPIENI DI NOCI E DATTER

# *Fried Ravioli Filled with Walnuts and Dates*

MAKES APPROX. 30 BISCUITS

I think it is amazing to take a recipe from just under a thousand years ago, cook it today and really enjoy it as our ancestors did. Originally this recipe was made just with a fig and walnut stuffing, which works well but if you like to experiment, as we do, try dates for natural sweetness, a grating of orange zest or a touch of spice such as cinnamon and pepper. If you use dates you may not need the honey at the end as they will probably be sweet enough. These come from the same period as the Sesame and Honey Biscuits on the opposite page and, like them, would be delicious with coffee or a sweet wine. See photo overleaf.

Sunflower or groundnut oil, for frying

10 tablespoons honey for coating the pastries (optional)

### FOR THE PASTRY

200 g (7 oz / 1 2/3 cups) '00' or plain (all-purpose) flour, plus extra for dusting

60 ml (2 fl oz) extra-virgin olive oil

90 ml (3 fl oz) water

### FOR THE FILLING

150 g (5 oz) dried figs or soft dates, stoned (approx. 12)

90 g (3 oz) walnuts

1 teaspoon freshly ground black pepper (optional)

1/2 teaspoon ground cinnamon (optional)

1/2 teaspoon finely grated orange zest (optional)

#### METHOD

Make the pastry by combining the flour, olive oil and water in a large mixing bowl. Knead until you have a smooth dough, adding a touch more water or flour if needed. Gather up into a ball, cover and chill for 30 minutes. While the dough is resting, finely grind all the filling ingredients together in a food processor.

Roll out the pastry as thinly as possible on a floured work surface, then cut into rounds with an 8 cm (3 in) cutter. Put 1 teaspoon of the filling on to a round and fold in half to make a semi-circle. If the edges don't stick together first time, brush on a little water to help. Pinch the edges together and continue making all the ravioli with the remaining dough and filling. Use a fork to make indentations to seal them further.

Fill a large saucepan halfway with oil and heat the oil until a piece of bread sizzles straight away when dropped in it. Fry the pastries, in batches if necessary so you don't overcrowd the pan, for 3–4 minutes or until crisp and golden. Remove with a slotted spoon and drain on kitchen paper. Warm the honey in a frying pan, if using, and bathe the pastries in it. Lift out with a slotted spoon and serve on a warm platter.

SESAME & HONEY BISCUITS,
PAGE 214

**FRIED RAVIOLI FILLED WITH WALNUTS & DATES, PAGE 215**

BACI DI COCCO

# *Coconut Kisses*

MAKES APPROX. 20 KISSES

As coconut is naturally sweet we have reduced the sugar right down to the minimum. These biscuits are also gluten free so you can indulge those who are intolerant. They are very moreish however, especially when still warm from the oven. If you really want to pipe the biscuits, blend the mixture of ingredients so that the coconut pieces are fine enough to pass through the nozzle. Much easier, however, is to form little mounds of coconut mixture with your hands.

### METHOD

Heat the oven to 160°C (320°F/ Gas 4) and line a baking tray with baking parchment. In a mixing bowl, beat the egg whites with a hand-held blender until stiff peaks form, then fold in the rest of the ingredients. The mixture will form into a paste. Pipe using a star nozzle, or use your hands to form walnut-size mounds of the mixture on to the baking tray, spaced around 3 cm (1 in) apart. Bake in the oven for 18–20 minutes or until golden brown. Remove from the oven and allow to cool on a wire rack. Store in an airtight container for up to 1 week.

3 egg whites
(approx. 80 g/3 oz)

150 g (5 oz)
desiccated
coconut

50 g (2 oz)
butter, melted

30 g (1 oz) caster
(superfine) sugar

1 teaspoon
vanilla extract

Small pinch of salt

TOZZETTI

# *Cinnamon and Hazelnut Biscuits*

MAKES 36–40 BISCUITS

These crunchy cinnamon and hazelnut biscuits are brittle like *cantuccini* (which outside of Italy are sometimes called by the general Italian name for biscuits '*biscotti*') making them ideal for dunking into coffee, tea or sweet wine. They have a definite Christmassy feel and make an ideal gift as they last for weeks once cooked. They are from Lazio where hazelnuts grow in abundance, but you can make them equally well with almonds or walnuts.

150 g (5 oz) hazelnuts

250 g (9 oz/2 cups) '00' or plain (all-purpose) flour

100 g (4 oz/ generous 1/2 cup) caster (superfine) sugar

50 g (2oz/generous 1/3 cup) icing (confectioners') sugar, plus extra for dusting

2 teaspoons ground cinnamon

2 teaspoon baking powder

2 eggs, beaten

Pinch of salt

Finely grated zest of 1/2 lemon

METHOD

Heat the oven to 180°C (350°F/Gas 6). Toast the hazelnuts in a single layer on a baking tray in the oven for around 6–8 minutes, being careful not to let them burn. Remove from the oven and tip on to a large plate or tray to cool.

Line a baking tray with baking parchment. Mix all the ingredients together by hand in a large bowl or in a stand mixer with a dough hook until you have a ball of dough. Lightly dust your work surface with icing (confectioners') sugar and turn the dough out on to it. Roll into 2 long flattened sausages measuring around 30 cm (12 in) long by 5 cm (2 in) wide. Lift the sausages on to the lined tray and bake in the oven for around 20 minutes or until firm to the touch. Remove from the oven and transfer to a cooking rack with a palette knife. Allow to cool for around 10 minutes.

Cut the sausages into 1 cm (½ in) slices with a large sharp knife. Lay the tozzetti back on to the lined oven tray and return to the oven for 5–10 minutes to dry out and crisp up. Remove from the oven and transfer to a wire rack to cool. When cool, store in an airtight container for up to 2 weeks.

# Tiramisu Three Ways

Tiramisu is everywhere around the world and we have tried to resist the temptation for including yet another recipe for it. However, Romans treat tiramisu as a staple Roman dessert (though the recipe probably originated in the Treviso in northern Italy) and they even have a chain of shops called Pompi: Home of the Tiramisu, where they serve a variety of flavours. Our visit there inspired me to include the best Roman version from our friend Ginevra and come up with our own versions of these popular creamy desserts. Giancarlo's tip for making a perfect tiramisu is to dunk the biscuits for just enough time to get them soaked but not soggy, then hold them vertically for a few seconds, giving them a gentle squeeze, to drain the excess coffee.

# GINEVRA'S TIRAMISU

SERVES 6

4 eggs, separated

4 tablespoons caster (superfine) sugar

500 g (1 lb 2 oz) mascarpone

12 *savoiardi* (ladyfinger) or *Pavesini* biscuits

300 ml (10 fl oz) cold espresso coffee

Cocoa powder for dusting

This one is for Giorgio, our son, who will eat all six tumblers if we let him.

*Ginevra Lovatelli*

GUEST RECIPE

**METHOD**

In a large bowl, beat the egg yolks with the sugar until pale. Whisk in the mascarpone until you have a smooth consistency without any lumps. In a separate bowl, use a hand-held blender to whip up the egg whites until you have firm peaks like snow. Gently fold the whipped egg whites into the mascarpone mixture and set aside.

Soak the biscuits one by one in the coffee for a few seconds then hold them vertically over the bowl and gently squeeze out the excess liquid. Break the biscuits in half and put them on a plate. When you have soaked all the biscuits, put half of them into the bottom of 6 glass tumblers. Divide half of the mascarpone mixture between each glass, spooning it over the biscuit layer. Layer over the remaining dunked biscuits followed by a final layer of mascarpone. Keep chilled. Just before serving, dust with a little cocoa powder.

---

# BANOFFEE MEETS TIRAMISU

SERVES 6

250 g (9 oz) mascarpone

25 g (1 oz/scant 1/4 cup) icing (confectioners') sugar

4 egg whites

12 *savoiardi* (ladyfinger) biscuits

100 ml (3 1/2 fl oz) Amaretto liqueur

100 ml (3 1/2 fl oz) water

1 x 397 g (14 oz) tin Carnation caramel or *dulce di leche*

6 small bananas

3 *Amaretti* biscuits

Sussex girl (me) meets Italian (Giancarlo) and so 'banamisu' is born. Did you know banoffee pie comes from the Hungry Monk restaurant in Sussex? Not many people do, but it was there that the wonderful combination of sticky boiled condensed milk, bananas and biscuits was conceived. I went in my teens and loved this now famous pie. This is a quick-to-throw-together, heavenly, rich pudding that combines the lightness of tiramisu with banoffee, and fuses my favourite English and Italian flavours together.

**METHOD**

Beat the mascarpone and sugar together in a large bowl. Whisk the egg whites in a separate bowl with a hand-held blender until they form stiff peaks. Add a couple of heaped tablespoons of the egg whites to the mascarpone and whisk in to loosen the mixture. Fold in the rest of the egg whites with a spatula until you have a light frothy cream. Set aside.

Mix together the Amaretto and water in a bowl. Dip the *savoiardi* biscuits, one at a time, into the liquid to soak them. Then hold the biscuit vertically for a few seconds to let it drain and gently squeeze; place the biscuit on to a plate and continue soaking the rest of the biscuits. Break all the soaked biscuits in half and then pour over a single layer of them into the bottom of 6 glass tumblers. Beat the caramel with a spoon to loosen it, then pour a 1 cm (1/2 in) layer over the biscuits. Slice the bananas and lay a single layer of them on to the caramel. Top with a layer of the mascarpone cream and then repeat the layers until the ingredients are used up. Chill in the fridge for at least an hour or up to overnight. Crumble the *Amaretti* biscuits on top just before serving.

# CHOCOLATE ORANGE TIRAMISU

SERVES 6

This decadent and rich dessert takes a little preparation but it's worth it, and it's even better when made the day before you need it. Make it with a liqueur, such as Grand Marnier or rum, and dark (bittersweet) chocolate for a grown-up version, or choose milk chocolate and freshly squeezed orange juice for a child-friendly one. If you would prefer to omit the uncooked egg white use whipping cream instead of the mascarpone mixture.

12 *savoiardi* (ladyfinger) or *Pavesini* biscuits

100 ml (3½ fl oz) Grand Marnier, rum or brandy, or use 200 ml (7 fl oz) orange juice and omit the water

100 ml (3½ fl oz) cold water

8 tablespoons orange marmalade

50 g (2 oz) dark (bittersweet) chocolate to serve

**FOR THE CHOCOLATE CUSTARD**

Use recipe on page 227 but half the quantities

**FOR THE MASCARPONE CREAM**

250 g (9 oz) mascarpone

25 g (1 oz/scant ¼ cup) icing (confectioners') sugar

4 egg whites

**METHOD**

First make the chocolate custard following the method on page 227.

To make the mascarpone cream, beat the mascarpone and icing (confectioners') sugar together in a large bowl. In a separate bowl, whisk the egg whites until they form stiff peaks. Add a couple of heaped tablespoons of whites to the mascarpone and whisk it in to loosen the mixture. Fold in the rest of the whites with a metal spoon until you have a light frothy cream. Set aside.

Now assemble the tiramisu. Soak the biscuits one by one in a mixture of your chosen alcohol and water, or the orange juice; after soaking, hold each biscuit vertically and gently squeeze out the excess liquid before placing on a plate. Break the biscuits into half, then put a single layer of them in the bottom of 6 glass tumblers. Spread some of the marmalade over the biscuits, followed by a layer of chocolate custard and a layer of the mascarpone. Repeat this layering until all the ingredients have been used up, ending with the mascarpone. Put into the fridge to chill for at least 1 hour and up to overnight. Before serving, grate over the chocolate.

GINEVRA'S TIRAMISU,
PAGE 221

CHOCOLATE ORANGE
TIRAMISU, PAGE 222

BANOFFEE MEETS
TIRAMISU, PAGE 221

**Dolci**

CREMA PASTICERA AL CIOCCOLATO

# Chocolate Custard

**SERVES 6-8** (makes 500 ml/17 fl oz)

Custard making is not hard and once mastered can be made quickly and easily rendering a silky smooth result. Use good quality chocolate, either milk or dark for the best flavour. This is used in the Chocolate Orange Tiramisu on page 222, but it is also wonderful with sliced banana and whipped cream for an indulgent dessert.

## METHOD

Heat the milk and vanilla in a medium saucepan over a medium heat until little bubbles form on the surface. Meanwhile, beat together the egg yolks, cornflour and sugar with a wooden spoon until smooth. Add a ladleful of hot milk to the beaten egg mixture and whisk immediately. Pour this mixture back into the pan containing the rest of the milk and bring to a gentle boil while stirring continuously with a wooden spoon. As soon as it thickens, remove the pan from the heat and stir in the chocolate pieces until completely melted into the custard, then transfer the custard to a cold bowl. Cover the surface of the custard with damp baking parchment to prevent a skin forming. Allow to cool with the vanilla pod, if using, still in the bowl. When the custard has cooled, discard the vanilla pod.

500 ml (17 fl oz) whole milk

$1/2$ vanilla pod or $1/2$ teaspoon vanilla extract

4 egg yolks

30 g (1 oz) cornflour (corn starch)

50 g (2 oz/$1/4$ cup) caster (superfine) sugar

100 g ($3^1/2$ oz) dark (bittersweet) chocolate (min. 70% cocoa solids), broken into small pieces

TORTA SBRICIOLONA RIPIENA DI RICOTTA AL LIMONE E LAMPONE

# Crumble Cake with Lemony Ricotta Filling and Raspberries

SERVES 10–12

I have a confession to make, I wanted to give you the perfect recipe for a typical Roman Jewish pastry tart, which encases sweet ricotta and the bitter cherry called *visciole*. However, after many attempts I had to admit defeat: it just wasn't 'nice'. Then I ate it again and again in Rome, and realised that I actually didn't like it there either. It's too sweet and, anyway, it's hard to find the right ricotta and the right cherries outside Italy. So here is our version which, in my humble opinion, is a much more user-friendly and ultimately more delicious version of the Roman ricotta and cherry pie.

## FOR THE CRUMBLE PASTRY

200 g (7 oz) unsalted butter

500 g (1 lb 2 oz / 4 cups) '00' or plain (all-purpose) flour

200 g (7 oz / 1¼ cups) icing (confectioners') sugar

1 teaspoon baking powder

Pinch of salt

2 eggs, beaten

1 vanilla pod seeds or 1 teaspoon vanilla extract

## FOR THE FILLING

600 g (1 lb 5 oz) ricotta

Finely grated zest of 1 lemon

2 tablespoons rum

1 teaspoon ground cinnamon

4 tablespoons caster (superfine) sugar

1 egg

250 g (9 oz) raspberries

300 ml (10 fl oz) whipping cream, whipped with 1 tablespoon icing (confectioners')

Sugar, to serve

## METHOD

Heat the oven to 180°C (350°F/ Gas 6) and line a 24 cm (9½ in) tart tin with baking parchment. Make the crumble pastry by rubbing the butter into the flour in a large bowl with your fingertips. Mix in icing (confectioners') sugar, baking powder and salt. Add the beaten eggs and vanilla seeds or extract and gradually mix then together, all the time rubbing the mixture together between your fingertips to create a crumble rather than one solid piece of dough. Scatter just over half of the mixture into the base of the lined tart tin. Press it down a little on to the base and up the sides of the tin to create a pastry shell. It doesn't have to be flat; bumpy is fine.

Mix together the ingredients for the filling, except for the raspberries. Gently fold in half the raspberries, leaving the rest to serve with the cake. Spoon the filling into the pastry shell and even it out with a spatula. Scatter over the remaining pastry to form a crust. Bake in the oven for 25 minutes or until golden. Serve with a bowl of lightly sweetened whipped cream and the remaining raspberries.

Variation: For a wicked cheat's – and actually rather delicious – filling, mix 200 g (7 oz) Nutella or chocolate spread with 600 g (1 lb 5 oz) ricotta, and fill the pie with this mixture rather than the lemony version. Cook for the same amount of time.

# *Ice creams & Sorbets*

Ice and fruit combos have been available in Rome for over 2,000 years. It seems Romans have loved the idea of chilled desserts since ancient times, when hot summers were made bearable for the likes of Nero with iced wine. The early emperors, before the birth of Christ, sent slaves to bring ice from the Apennine mountains to Rome so that it could be mixed with fruit and honey, to the delight of their guests. It was stored in ice houses using straw as insulation and could last for months. Nero is recorded by ancient authors as having invented a system for ice-cooling sterilised water, by boiling it first and then chilling it instantly in snow. This was very costly and was only added to the finest wine. Rome still has this combination of ice and fruit in the form of *grattachecca*, literally 'shaved ice' mixed with sugary syrups sold from kiosks along the Tiber in summer. My favourite flavour is amarena cherries in their syrup and pieces of coconut.

The art of *gelato* – Italian ice cream – making is taken very seriously and enthusiasts seek out artisan makers who refuse to use pre-mixed ingredients. Some of the best that we visited are Fatamorgana, Carapina, Bar Giolitti, Gracchi and Il Gelato di Claudio Torcè. If you see huge piles of whipped-up brightly coloured ice creams you are buying air that is whipped in to increase the volume, artificial colours and flavours, so walk away. Proper *gelato* is flat in the serving tubs, and look for the pistachio flavour and ask yourself if it looks like it came from the nut, i.e. greenish brown in colour, or is it bright minty green and full of E-numbers?

SORBETTO ALLA PESCA

# *Whole Peach Sorbet*

SERVES 6-8

Inspired by Fatamorgana, the amazing artisan *gelateria* who make a peaches in white wine flavour sorbet, I made this recipe. I like to serve it topped with ice-cold Prosecco, but it is equally good the way our son Flavio likes it: served in frosted tall glasses with whipped cream, strawberries and more slices of peach. I have to confess our peaches were not perfectly ripe and so the skins were really hard to peel off. We decided to leave them on, which alters the purity of colour but actually doesn't harm the flavour at all. I would say find ripe peaches and remove the skin if you can, but if not blitz away and enjoy the time saved from peeling!

## METHOD

Peel and stone the peaches. If the skin is very hard to remove or time is short it can be left on, but the result will be slightly speckled. Blitz the pulp in a food processor to a purée. Pour the purée into a saucepan and mix in the sugar and lemon juice. Heat until the sugar is dissolved, then remove from the heat and pour into a bowl to cool to room temperature. Churn in an ice cream machine or follow the method for making sorbet by hand on page 240.

900 g (2 lb) peaches

100 g (3$^1$/$_2$ oz/ scant $^1$/$_2$ cup) caster (superfine) sugar

Juice of $^1$/$_2$ lemon

SORBETTO AL CIOCCOLATO

# Chocolate Sorbet

SERVES 8–10

There is something a little naughty and definitely enticing about the deep-red interior and its appealing array of glistening chocolates in Confetteria Moriondo e Gariglio, a chocolate shop in Rome established in 1886. In a room looking more like a lady's cosy boudoir than a shop, fresh chocolates are made daily according to a family recipe. We were told by the manager that a century ago well-dressed ladies came in to buy their favourite indulgences and now their grandchildren come in to continue the tradition. It reminded us of Joanne Harris's Chocolat, where chocolates become the magical cure-all to the ailing customers. Apparently all the customers have their favourites and the staff take pleasure in knowing who likes what.

Inspired by our visit here and some pleasantly bitter espresso at Sciascia Caffe, photographed here, we have combined the two flavours in this luxurious chocolate sorbet. Eat it naked or clothed in sweetened whipped cream, or even in a small glass doused in a hot espresso.

150 g (5 oz) dark (bittersweet) chocolate (min. 70% cocoa solids), finely chopped, plus extra to serve

400 ml (13 fl oz) water

200 ml (7 fl oz) strong black coffee

200 g (7 oz/ generous 3/4 cup) caster (superfine) sugar

100 g (3 1/2 oz) best-quality fine cocoa powder

300 ml (10 fl oz) whipping cream, whipped to soft peaks, to serve (optional)

METHOD

Heat the chocolate in the microwave or in a glass bowl over a saucepan of boiling water (make sure the bowl doesn't touch the surface of the water). Meanwhile, whisk together the water, coffee, sugar and cocoa powder in a saucepan over a medium heat. When both mixtures are hot and smooth, pour the melted chocolate into the coffee mixture and whisk thoroughly to combine. Remove from the heat and pour into a clean bowl to cool. When cold, churn in an ice-cream machine or follow the method of making sorbet by hand on page 240. Serve in cold glasses with whipped cream and grated bitter chocolate.

# *Tropical Fruit Salad*

SERVES 2

1 mango

200 g (7 oz) pineapple pieces

1 papaya

1 banana

2 passion fruits

Use any tropical fruit available such as mango, grapes, pineapple, papaya, passion fruit and pomegranate seeds. If time is short, use the pre-cut packs of exotic fruit rather than whole fruits for the selection and speed. For easy entertaining we have glasses of this ready in the fridge, spooning over a heap of Pineapple and Ginger Granita (see below) just before serving.

**METHOD**

Peel and cut the fruit into bite-size pieces. Gently combine with the seeds of the passion fruits and arrange in martini or wine glasses. Apart from the banana, this can be done up to 2 hours in advance and chilled in the fridge – add the banana just before serving. To serve, top with a few tablespoons of Pineapple and Ginger Granita (see below) and eat straight away.

---

# *Pineapple and Ginger Granita*

SERVES 6–8

50 g (2 oz) fresh ginger

75 g (2 1/2 oz/scant 1/3 cup) caster (superfine) sugar

250 ml (8 1/2 fl oz) water

135 ml (4 1/2 fl oz) white rum

500 g (1 lb 2oz) pineapple, peeled and cut into chunks

Sweet and refreshing granita originally comes from Sicily and is a coarsely textured ice that cools you down in the summer heat. It is easy to make and doesn't require an ice cream machine. Pineapple and ginger is one of the flavours at Fatamorgana, one of Rome's imaginative artisan *gelaterie*. We have added a dash of white rum to the mix and kept the sugar low to avoid too much sweetness. The addition of alcohol also stops it setting too hard, which can happen in low-sugar concoctions. Try it on its own or with a generous spoonful of whipped and lightly sweetened cream.

**METHOD**

Scrape the skin from the ginger root and cut it into 5 mm (¼ in) thick slices. Put the slices into a small lidded saucepan with the sugar and water, and bring to the boil. Reduce to a gentle heat and simmer with the lid on for 10 minutes. Remove the pan from the heat and leave to cool. Blitz the ginger, the cooking liquor, rum and the pineapple together in a food processor for several minutes or until you have a smooth purée. Pour the purée into a freezer-proof container and freeze for about 1 hour or until the mixture has just started to freeze around the edges. Remove from the freezer and use a fork to break up and mix the frozen bits in with the less-frozen middle parts. Put back in the freezer and after 30 minutes repeat the process of breaking up the frozen bits into the less-frozen parts. Continue freezing and breaking up the mixture until the whole mixture is made up of small frozen ice crystals. Alternatively, use an ice-cream maker but the result will be smooth.

Variation: The Wonky Madonna cocktail mix on page 244 will also freeze into a spicy granita; simply make up the syrup and freeze as above.

GELATO ALLA CREMA

# Rich Custard Ice Cream Base

MAKES 700 ML (23 1/2 FL OZ)

This recipe is inspired by the *gelaterie* of Rome, particularly the inventive flavours found in the artisan *gelaterie*, such as Fatamorgana which had combinations like pear and gorgonzola, and banana with black sesame. This base makes the kind of really smooth and heavenly ice cream that they serve in Italian *gelaterie*. Proper *gelato* is lower in fat than the ice cream we're used to, and this is achieved by using more milk than cream and less eggs than a standard ice cream recipe. Once you have mastered making a custard base like this you can add the flavourings suggested below or have fun experimenting with your own. You will need an ice-cream maker or use the method on page 240 for churning by hand.

## METHOD

In a large saucepan, heat the milk and cream with half the sugar over a medium heat until just bubbling. Meanwhile, in a large bowl beat together the egg yolks and remaining sugar until smooth. Add 2 ladlefuls of hot milk to the egg mixture and immediately whisk together. Pour this back into the pan and whisk everything together until thickened.

To sterilise the ice cream, turn up the heat and increase the temperature of the mixture to 85°C (185°F). This is the point when the ice cream coats the back of a spoon if you don't have a thermometer. Take off the heat immediately and pour into a large heatproof bowl. To cool quickly, set this bowl over another bowl full of iced water, and then cover the surface of the custard with damp baking parchment to stop a skin from forming. Stir every so often to help it cool evenly. As soon as the custard is at room temperature, churn in an ice-cream machine or by hand using the method on page 240.

400 ml (13 fl oz) whole (full-fat) milk

250 ml (8 1/2 fl oz) double (heavy) cream

100 g (3 1/2 oz /scant 1/2 cup) caster (superfine) sugar

4 egg yolks

# *Flavour Suggestions*

### VANILLA ICE CREAM

Add 1 teaspoon of vanilla extract or the seeds scraped from 1 vanilla pod to the egg and sugar mixture before mixing with the hot milk. Cool and churn as before.

### TOASTED HAZELNUT ICE CREAM

Add 100 g (3½ oz) toasted hazelnuts that have been blitzed to a rough sandy texture in a food processor to the custard before churning. Any nuts are good, but do toast them first to bring out the flavour in the natural oils.

### CHOCOLATE AND GRAND MARNIER ICE CREAM

Add 100 g (3½ oz) dark (bittersweet) chocolate (min. 70% cocoa solids), broken into small pieces, into the hot custard, off the heat, as soon as it thickens. Stir in 135 ml (4½ fl oz) of Grand Marnier, then cool and churn as before.

### HERB ICE CREAM

Aromatic herbs such as mint, rosemary, lemon balm and basil make wonderful delicately flavoured ice creams that are perfectly acceptable on their own but will also make the perfect partner to other desserts. Try combinations such as the Roman Apple Cake on page 208 with rosemary flavoured ice cream, or try basil ice cream with fresh strawberries, and mint ice cream with any chocolate tart.

To make herb ice cream, infuse 10 g (½ oz) of herbs (leave them whole; you don't need to chop them up) in the milk and cream overnight to make the ice cream the next day. Strain the infused mixture through a sieve and use this instead of the plain milk and cream when you make the custard for the ice cream. If you are in a hurry and can't leave the herbs to infuse overnight, double the quantity of herbs and put them into the milk and cream. Bring to the boil as before and then allow to cool and infuse the milk for 1 hour before straining and making the custard as before.

### MAKING ICE CREAM AND SORBETS WITHOUT AN ICE-CREAM MACHINE

If you don't have an ice-cream machine, when the custard or sorbet base is cool, pour it into a freezer-proof shallow container and put it into the freezer. Whisk the mixture every hour for 4 hours to break down the ice crystals as they form. When it has all frozen it is ready to eat, or cover and leave for another day. Another way is to freeze the mixture in ice cube trays or small yoghurt pots and, when frozen, tip the contents into a food processor and blend to break up the ice crystals. Cover and freeze again straight away before it has a chance to melt. This is the quickest and easiest way to do it, and it results in a smooth *gelato*, but you do need space in your freezer and a good food processor to do it.

# Cocktails

It would be impossible to summarise Rome's buzzing nightlife in a couple of paragraphs, but out of our many trips there two bars shone out through the dark of the night and attracted us like moths to the flame. First, The Jerry Thomas Project, a dimly lit speakeasy in central Rome, now rated one of the best bars in the world. Its red lacquered walls and damask gold print wallpapers make you feel like you are in an opium den, until you see the shelves displaying years of liquor collection and obsession. The original Jerry Thomas wrote the famous cocktail recipe book *How to Mix Drinks*, also known as *The Bon Vivant's Companion*, in 1862. For many, including Leonardo Leuci, it has been a bible and was the inspiration for his outstanding bar hidden away in a backstreet of Rome. You need to know the answer to a cocktail related question on their website to get in or get on the guest list. Leonardo likes to show off Italy's forgotten spirits and his mind-blowing concoctions are prepared by bearded men in waistcoats who look like they are straight out of 1920s New York.

Secondly, we love the Akbar in Trastevere, whose eclectic and inviting interior pulls you off the street and into a bar-cum-restaurant that breaks tradition by serving cocktails and food. We loved the *aperitivo* evenings where you can eat inexpensively from a buffet.

Roman bars have been in existence for over 2,000 years. In 4th century BC there was already a grid of streets with bars that had counters and mosaic pictorial menus for the illiterate. Signs for these popinae were painted with symbols, like the 'three cups', so they were easily recognised, and this was the origins of modern pub signs. People stood to eat or sat on stools and benches. So don your toga, pour yourself one of the following cocktails and serve some of the antipasti such as the *Globi* (Cheese and Honey Pastries) on page 69, the Hot Fish Pickle on page 63 with creamy ricotta on crispy *Lagana* (see page 62), or a slice of *Pizza Bianca Romana* on page 61.

# The Wonky Madonna

MAKES 8–10 COCKTAILS

Inspired by a tilted picture of a rather demure Madonna in a cocktail bar, this is a sweet, innocent-tasting drink with a hidden kick of chilli and alcohol. To make a non-alcoholic version, remove the Grand Marnier from the recipe, add a little sugar for sweetness and top up with tonic or soda water instead of Prosecco. The spiced orange juice needs to be made the day before you want to serve the cocktail, to allow the flavours to infuse. If you buy the juice make sure it is only juice and doesn't contain any other flavours or additives.

1 bottle Prosecco

FOR THE SPICED
ORANGE JUICE

300 ml (10 fl oz) freshly squeezed blood orange juice (either from fruits or a chilled carton)

200 ml (7 fl oz) water

3 x 8 cm (3 in) strips of orange zest (use a potato peeler to peel off the strips)

5 tablespoons Grand Marnier, Cointreau or brandy

1 small dried red chilli or 1/2 fresh chilli

1 x 5 cm (2 in) cinnamon stick

1 star anise

3 cardamom pods, lightly crushed

TO SERVE
(OPTIONAL)

Star anise

Small cinnamon sticks

Slices of orange

METHOD

To make the spiced orange juice, put all of the ingredients into a medium saucepan and bring to the boil. Cook for a couple of minutes and crush the spices gently with a wooden spoon. Remove from the heat and allow to cool to room temperature. Cover and chill in the fridge overnight to infuse the flavours.

Pour the cooled juice through a sieve into a jug and chill. When you are ready to serve, pour 50 ml (2 fl oz) of the Spiced Orange Juice into each Champagne or cocktail glass over a couple of ice cubes and top with Prosecco. Decorate the glass with orange slices, star anise and cinnamon sticks if you like.

# *Hugo*

In the wonderfully eccentric Akbar in Trastevere, they serve Hugo in bowl glasses so big you want to dive in and swim around in concentric circles with your mouth open. After a hard day's recipe hunting, it is a welcome and refreshing cocktail. Originally it was from Alto Adige in northern Italy, but now its popularity has spread over Italy. You can have a fairly innocent version with elderflower syrup and a splash of sparkling water, or enjoy a little more punch by using the elderflower liqueur called St-Germain. Buy it for the bottle alone; it looks like an elegant Art Deco skyscraper.

## METHOD

To make one Hugo take a few ice cubes, 50 ml (2 fl oz) of elderflower syrup or St-Germain, 125 ml (4 fl oz) Prosecco or sparkling wine, a few mint leaves and slice of lime, and put it all in a big glass. Stir together and drink straight away.

# *Negroni*

In 1919 Count Negroni stood at the bar of the Caffè Giacosa in Florence (which is now called Caffè Cavalli, in case you are thinking of visiting) and ordered the barman to improve his Americano by adding gin. He did so and also added a twist of orange, and it became known as the Negroni. Count Negroni and family were so impressed they set up a factory producing the drink in ready-mixed form known as Antico Negroni. No one is entirely sure if this is in fact its true origin, but it's a good story and, apparently, Orson Welles said of the new drink in 1947, 'The bitters are excellent for your liver, the gin is bad for you. They balance each other!'

**METHOD**

Take 30 ml (1 fl oz) gin, 30 ml (1 fl oz) red vermouth, 30 ml (1 fl oz) Campari and stir together with a slice of orange and a few ice cubes.

**VARIATION: NEGRONI *SBAGLIATO***

The word *sbagliato* means 'mistaken' or 'wrong', as in this cocktail the gin in the standard Negroni (above) is replaced with a splash of Prosecco.

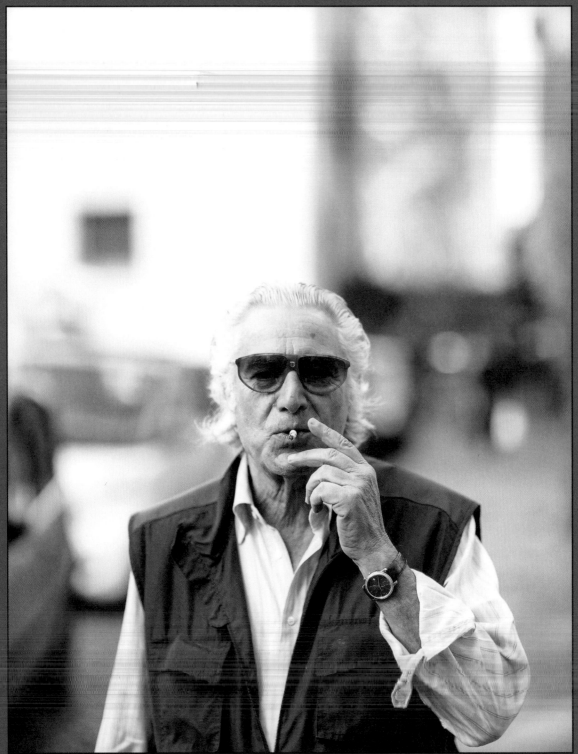

# Let the Romans Speak

During our trips to Rome to research recipes for this book, we spoke to many wonderful chefs there who were kind enough to share some of their favourite recipes with us. We talked to them about what they believe makes Roman food so special, and we want to share some of their thoughts with you so that you can get to know them a little too. In ancient Rome, gladiators were thrown a huge banquet in their honour and given a special meal of their choice the day before a fight, called a *cena libera*, which was potentially their last ever meal; we asked our modern day kitchen gladiators what theirs would be.

# Claudia Paiella

OWNER, ENOTECA CORSI

Enoteca Corsi originally opened its doors as a wine shop in the 1940s, specialising in the Tuscan wine Chianti – it still has *Chianti corsi* written over the main entrance. Claudia's first uncle opened the wine shop, but in the 1960s her father took it over and started serving local Roman 'fast food', like *burro e alici panini* (butter and anchovy sandwiches), eggs and delicious soups; he did something different every day. The restaurant grew in popularity and has since become the main draw of the old wine shop. These days, along with her parents and auntie and uncle, Claudia and her sister keep the tradition alive by serving fresh and tasty food using the same recipes and ingredients as when the restaurant started.

Claudia's last meal would consist of: fried cauliflower in *pastella* with a sprinkle of oil and anchovy *vinaigrette*; traditionally made chickpea soup; stewed cod fish with raisins, onions and fresh tomato (*baccalà alla romana*), the fish gently fried in the pan first and then baked in the oven; side dish of *puntarelle romane*; and finally for dessert a slice of incredible ricotta and wild cherry tart (*crostata ricotta e visciole*). Her favourite Roman ingredient is artichoke from the local area. She says it is 'amazing especially in March when you can find the best-quality artichoke to make the *carciofi alla romana*'. The dish that Claudia cooks most often at home is soup. 'I love soups made with spelt, barley, beans, peas and potatoes. These soups can be nice and hot in the winter and warm and fresh in the summer.' When we asked Claudia how she would describe Roman food, she said 'Simple but also mystical like Rome. Roman cooking is delicious, earthy and full of tradition: it never disappoints the people who live in Rome or those who pass through it.'

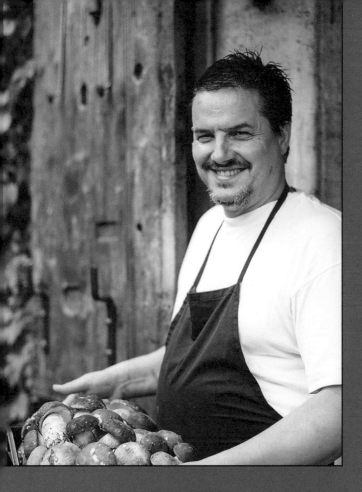

# Teodore Filippini

CHEF, DA TEO

Teo and his wife, Titziana, run Da Teo, a charming *trattoria* in Trastevere which is packed with locals and a few tourists in the know. He is passionate about using ingredients at their best and when we were there was furiously composing dishes with porcini and just-picked white truffles. His last supper would be grouper fish cooked with perfectly ripe tomatoes in the oven. At home his favourite meal for his family is deep fried breaded lamb cutlets with artichokes. At work he sources Roman *guanciale*, cured pig's cheek, to flavour his traditional dishes like carbonara and *amatriciana*. Roman food, he told us, is cooked from the heart; it is honest and packed with flavour from herbs and fantastic ingredients.

# Ginevra Lovatelli

ROMAN TOUR GUIDE

Ginevra is a friend and an expert on Rome; she was born and raised there, and is passionate about sharing Roman culture with others. She runs Secret Rome and wrote a book of the same name. Her favourite Roman ingredients are *mentuccia*, lesser calamint, and *carciofo romanesco*, Roman artichoke, but says her last supper would have to be either *tiramisu* or a very good *mozzarella di buffala*.

# Roberto Lisi and Davide Cianetti

OWNER & CHEF, PIERLUIGI

Pierluigi's owner Roberto's favourite meal is *pasta con vongole*, a dish made with clams, chilli and parsley. Even if he's in the restaurant, if he wants to eat this he makes it himself – he loves it made exactly his way. Roberto told me, 'The ingredients may be the same for everyone but the difference is the hand that makes it.'

Davide says that Roman cooking is '*vera*', meaning 'true'; it is full of tradition and authenticity – it respects the people. Davide is the son of a butcher and grew up wishing he could eat fillets like his friends, but his parents had to sell the best cuts to make money: 'To buy the jacket, he had to sell the fillet.' His last meal would be *pajata*, the intestine of a calf that has only been fed on its mother's milk cooked in tomato sauce, served with *rigatoni* pasta.

'The ingredients may be the same for everyone but the difference is the hand that makes it.'

# Silvia Nacamulli

COOKERY TEACHER

**What would be your last supper?**
It depends on the season as my taste buds change accordingly. In spring *carciofi alla Giudia*, in summer any dish with tomatoes, fresh vegetables and fruit, in autumn – or perhaps all year round! – *melanzane alla parmigiana* and in winter a great soup.

**What is your favourite Roman ingredient?**
*Carciofo Romanesco* or *Cimarolo* – Roman artichoke, available just for a few months a year but it is worth the wait!

**What is the dish you cook often at home for the family?**
Lots and lots of vegetables, mostly sautéed with either garlic or onion, or roasted. Courgettes, carrots, broccoli, spinach, chicory, aubergines, peppers – not cooked together, one at a time to taste its full flavour.

**How would you describe Roman food in a sentence?**
Soulful, traditional, home-cooking at its best. It respects all parts of animals and vegetables, also what most people would discard and creating delicious dishes from it.

# Micaela Pavoncello

ROMAN JEWISH TOUR GUIDE IN ROME

**What would be your last supper?**
A dinner based on fish; *antipasto di pescetti fritti di paranza* (small fried fish); *spaghetti aglio olio peperoncino e bottarga fresca* (spaghetti with garlic, oil, chilli and fresh bottaga); *carpaccio di spigola* (sebass *carpaccio*); and *sorbetto o gelato al limone* (sorbet or ice cream).

**What is your favourite Roman ingredient?**
*Pecorino Romano* cheese.

**What is the dish you cook often at home for the family?**
Pasta cacio e pepe e sogliola alla mugnaia (pasta with cheese and pepper and sole *meunière*).

**How would you describe Roman food in a sentence?**
*Povero e sublime* (poor and sublime).

# Alessandro Roscioli

CO-OWNER, ROSCIOLI

The Roscioli family place quality and tradition at the top of their priorities when it comes to Roman cuisine, which is seen in their restaurant, bakery and deli. We spoke to one of the sons, Alessandro, who runs the bakery Antico Forno Roscioli with his brother Pierluigi. Alessandro has a passion for tomatoes in all forms, cooked and raw, and his last meal would be *pasta al pomodoro*, pasta with tomatoes. He describes Roman cooking as, 'The real thing – no frills and not too many flavours.'

# Paolo Trancassini

OWNER, LA CAMPANA

When we visited La Campana, Paolo gave us a book about the origin of the restaurant, which is one of the oldest in Rome and has been standing here since 1518 – it even gave its name to the street it's on, Vicolo della Campana. Originally the restaurant was a staging post, where people on their travels would order a route and make a contract: Paolo has one from 1836 detailing a journey to Ancona hanging on the wall. People would make the contract, eat and drink and sleep the night, arising refreshed the next day to make the journey to the next staging post. Paolo, whose last supper would be of sweetbreads, feels that food hasn't changed much over recent years though dishes such as tripe have had a resurgence recently as people have turned to simple, traditional dishes away from the over-elaborate, more pretentious cooking in the media.

> '*Roman cooking is a kitchen of rich flavours and poor ingredients. It is a generous and light cuisine – because it doesn't miss anything.*'

## Stefania Menichetti

HOME COOK

Stefania is a busy mum and family friend who cooks three-ingredient dishes after a working day. When we asked Stefania how she would describe Roman food, she told us, 'Roman cooking is a kitchen of rich flavours and poor ingredients. It is a generous and light cuisine – because it doesn't miss anything.' Her favourite family meal is lamb *cacciatora*-style, which means 'hunter's wife', but her last supper would be a feast of fried courgette (zucchini) flowers, white lasagne with artichoke, *scottadito* lamb, sautéed chicory leaves, and finishing with apple cake. Her favourite Roman ingredient is artichoke.

## Arcangelo Dandini

OWNER & CHEF, SUPPLIZIO

Arcangelo's last supper would be *foie gras*, which has been in Rome since antiquity. Originally discovered by the ancient Egyptians, the ancient Romans brought it to Italy during their occupation of Egypt some 2,000 years ago, well before it was popularised by the French many years later. They also found that if you fed the geese figs and sweet wine, the taste would stay in the livers making the *foie gras* even more luxurious. Arcangelo says of Roman food, 'It has gone through the eras unscathed, always remaining original and keeping its identity, unchanged. '

Supplizio is Arcangelo's second restaurant and specialises in Roman street food.

# Maria Cristina Milozzi & Emanuele Maggio

OWNER & HEAD CHEF, AL CEPPO

Al Ceppo is an old, established restaurant in Rome, which uses a beautiful old grill to cook over. Opened in 1964, it is run by Maria and her daughter Caterina and has become an institution. *Ceppo* means a stump of wood; you are as long-lasting as a *ceppo*!

Maria brings her herbs in from home and is fastidious about the dishes served. She thinks that traditional flavours give you comfort and security, and it's the traditional dishes that most people like. At the same time, she believes you can add new twists to old dishes, such as a pork fillet with ginger and pumpkin; the key is to not overcomplicate dishes by mixing too many flavours, which is what spoils it. Maria's last supper would be *carbonara,* made properly with only egg yolks and no cream, or *amatriciana*, a simple spaghetti dish with cured pork cheeks *(guanciale)* and a tomato sauce.

Emanuele's last meal would also be a simple and traditional dish, *cacio e pepe* – pasta with cheese and pepper. He says, 'Roman cooking is from the heart. It is a poor man's cooking, with flavour.'

'Roman cooking is from the heart. It is a poor man's cooking, with flavour.'

# Wendy Holloway

FOOD GUIDE & COOKERY TEACHER

Originally from Pittsburgh, Pennsylvania, Wendy has now lived in Rome for over thirty years and runs the culinary experience company Flavours of Italy. Wendy told us that it has always been easy to get fresh food in Rome, both in terms of what is grown locally but also what is imported. However, in her opinion it is unforgiveable not to have the seasonal food that is on offer; the fish comes in daily from the sea and the nearby mountains supply many locally grown ingredients. Wendy's last supper would be her home cooked *spaghetti alla carbonara*, using her favourite Roman ingredient *guanciale,* cured pork cheeks.

# Anna Davies

HOME COOK

**What would be your last supper?**
Pasta and *ceci* (chickpeas) with an overload of garlic.

**What is your favourite Roman ingredient?**
Rosemary, we use it for everything. Roast potatoes, white pizza, beans and chickpeas.

**What is the dish you cook often at home for the family?**
I make pasta every day with whatever I have in the fridge. Lemon pasta is super easy: grated lemon, olive oil, parmesan and a drop of single cream. I get veggies from the market in front of my house and base our food on them. We don't eat a lot of meat and Tuesdays and Fridays is always fish! Pasta with pepperoni or broccoli or *rape* (turnip) or artichoke. I make a sort of pesto with yellow (bell) peppers that can go on *bruschetta* or on pasta.

**How would you describe Roman food in a sentence?**
Roman food is simple, tasty and seasonal. You don't need a calendar, just see what veggies are on the menu. Today I have already prepared broccoli, turnips and my favourite food ever *puntarelle* (a local chicory).

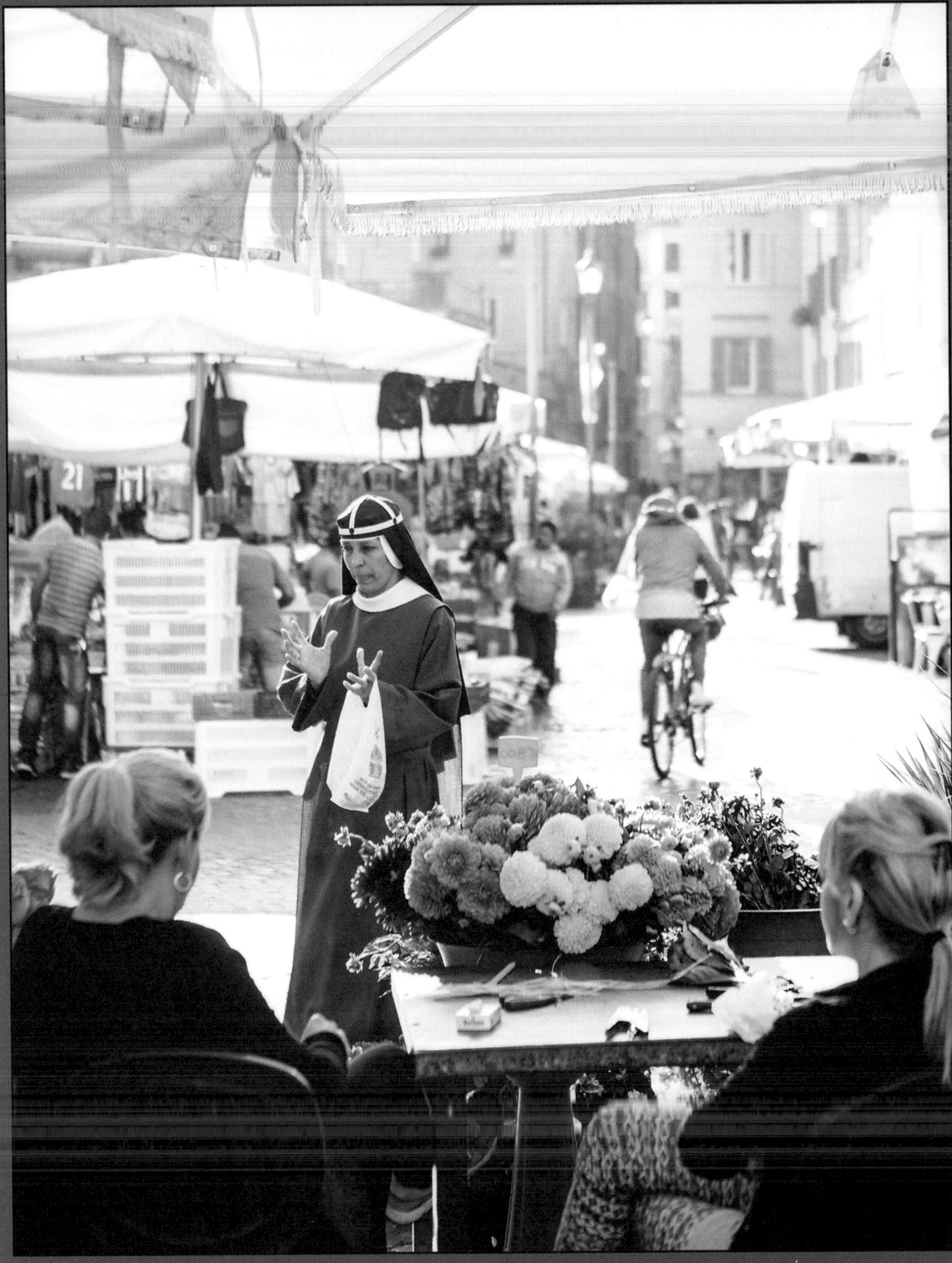
21

# Grazie,
# Thank you

**KATE POLLARD,
PUBLISHER**

For your continued belief in us and
your perpetual support, we really
love working with you and Helen.

**HELEN CATHCART,
PHOTOGRAPHER**

Our third book together and
your photos still wow us.

**KAJAL MISTRY,
SENIOR EDITOR**

For your patience, care and
attention while putting
this book together.

**SUSAN PEGG,
COPY EDITOR**

For your meticulous care
and thorough attention.

**JULIA MURRAY,
DESIGNER**

Thank you for your
inspiring designs, care
and attention to detail.

**WENDY HOLLOWAY,
ROMAN COOKERY TEACHER,
GUIDE & FRIEND**

For your generosity of knowledge,
wonderful food and home.

**STEFANIA MENICHETTI**

For your help, knowledge and
time, you are our Roman sister
and thank you for taking us to
your local restaurant Il Boccioni.

**GINEVRA LOVATELLI**

For showing us your secret Rome,
for unlocking doors, sharing your
knowledge and your lovely home.

**ANNE HUDSON**

For your kind help and research
on ancient Rome and relentless
enthusiasm for recipe testing.

**HANNAH PRICE,
CAMBRIDGE SCHOLAR &
ROMAN HISTORIAN**

For your detailed research
and guidance.

**CLAUDIA RODEN**

For your detailed advice on the
Roman Jewish traditions.

**SILVIA NACAMULLI**

For your time and
wonderful recipes.

**MARCELLO PAGLIAI, ADRIANO
FESTUCCIA, ITALO FORTE**

*Per essere i miei amici
di sempre.*

**ANNA DAVIES**

For teaching us your
fantastic family recipes.

**MICAELA PAVONCELLO**

For giving us such an insight
into Roman Jewish life.

**SHEILA ABELMAN,
LITERARY AGENT**

For consistently
looking after us.

**ANGELA RUOCCO**

For double-checking
the Italian.

**MANJULA SAMARASINGHE,
KAREN COURTNEY,
LIZ BENTHAM-CLARK**

Thank you for recipe testing
and read-throughs.

**AUBREY ALLEN BUTCHERS**

For your marvellous
butchery advice and
supply of unusual cuts.

**SAVANNA, GERRARDS CROSS**

Our lovely local butchers.

## Restaurants we recommend

**AKBAR, TRASTEVERE, WWW.AK-BAR.COM**

Delicious food and cocktails in this eclectic bar/restaurant

**AL CEPPO, PARIOLI, WWW.RISTORANTEALCEPPO.IT**

Fabulous restaurant with wonderful food, try anything cooked on the old open grill.

**DA SETTIMIO, TEL: +39 06 5823 0701**

I love this tiny trattoria run by husband and wife team, have the involtini (beef rolls).

**DA TEO, TRASTEVERE, WWW.TRATTORIADATEO.IT**

Teodore Filippine and his wife Tiziana run this fabulous little trattoria where locals dominate the crowd. Try the arrabbiata pasta and the polpettine di bollito. Say hi to Teo for us.

**DAR MOSCHINO, GARBATELLA, TEL: +39 06 513 9473**

A little out of the centre but worth the visit and favourable wine prices make up for the taxi fare. A true Roman trattoria down to the checked tablecloths and exceptional flavours.

**ENOTECA CORSI, VIA DEL GESU', WWW.ENOTECACORSI.COM**

Situated between the Pantheon and Piazza Venezia. Run by Romans to feed the Romans, a true traditional neighbourhood osteria. Try the soups and pasta. Say hi to Claudia for us.

**JERRY THOMAS PROJECT, WWW.THEJERRYTHOMASPROJECT.IT**

Check the website for the password. Visit this speakeasy for the best ever cocktails.

**LA CAMPANA, WWW.RISTORANTELACAMPANA.COM**

Proper traditional food at the oldest restaurant in central Rome – have the apple pie. Say hi to Paolo for us.

**LA TAVERNA DEL GHETTO, WWW.LATAVERNADELGHETTO.COM**

Traditional Jewish tavern. Try the plate of wilted tomatoes, the chef's bean dip and bread.

**MORDI E VAI, TESTACCIO MARKET**

Try the fried meat patties here.

**OSTERIA L'ARICCIAROLA, TEL: +39 06 933 4103**

Venture a little further out of town in Castelli to try the real porchetta meal.

**PIERLUIGI, WWW.PIERLUIGI.IT**

Dress up and enjoy spotting the celebs while you sit outside, drink bollicine (bubbles) and eat the freshest seafood or try the home-marinated thinly sliced beef and delicious pasta. Say hi to Roberto for us.

**PIZZA DA FORNO CAMPO DEI FIORI, WWW.FORNOCAMPODEFIORI.COM**

In our opinion the best pizza in town, which is strange given its tourist haven location on the market square. Watch them make it through the windows.

**RISTORANTE L'ARCANGELO, VIA GIUSEPPE GIOACCHINO BELLI,**

59 Arcangelo Dandini's, www.larcangelo.com Superb restaurant. Say hi to Arcangelo for us.

**ROSCIOLI, LA SALUMERIA, WWW.SALUMERIAROSCIOLI.COM**

Restaurant and deli and Il Forno bakery both near Campo de'Fiori. The best carbonara we ate was from here, wonderful selection of salumi and cheeses too. Say hi to Alessandro for us

**SCIASCIA CAFFE, VIA FABIO MASSIMO 80/A**

Wonderful old-fashioned café with amazing coffee served in perfect china cups. Try the granita of the day if you see it.

**SIBILLA, WWW.RISTORANTESIBILLA.COM**

Further still is Villa D'Este with a stunning house and gardens. book lunch or dinner at nearby Sibilla, you won't find a better backdrop for a meal.

**SORA MARGHERITA, TEL: +39 06 687 4216**

Wonderful, tiny restaurant situated in the Jewish Ghetto.

**SUPPLIZIO, WWW.SUPPLIZIO.NET**

Come here during the day for Dandini's amazing supplì and a beer. They won't be bettered.

**TRAPPIZZINO, WWW.TRAPIZZINO.IT**

Unusual triangular bread stuffed with amazing stews, supplì and snacks.

**VOLPETTI AND VOLPETTI PIU, TESTACCIO, WWW.VOLPETTI.COM**

Shop selling a huge variety of artisan cheeses, salumi and pastries. Down the road its café serves tavola calda dishes and wonderful pizza.

## Tours and Cookery Classes

**CINECITTÁ WORLD, WWW.CINECITTAWORLD.IT**

A fantastic new theme park if your kids are bored of the sights! Great rides and lovely food – so different from most theme parks.

**EATING ITALY, WWW.EATINGITALYFOODTOURS.COM**

Small group tours of Italy's cities, we loved our Testaccio tasting tour.

**FLAVORS OF ITALY, WWW.FLAVOROFITALY.COM**

Cookery classes, foodie tours and holidays run by charming expert and Rome resident Wendy Holloway.

**IMAGO ARTIS TOURS, WWW.IATRAVEL.COM**

Great in-depth tours of the city's major sights by specialists such as Caterina di Gregori.

**JEWISH ROMA WALKING TOURS, WWW.JEWISHROMA.COM**

Fascinating tours by Micaela Pavoncello and her team around the ghetto and other sights.

**SECRET ROME, WWW.SECRETROME.IT**

Ginevra Lovatelli's fascinating private art, history and food tours of Rome.

## Blogs we like

**BUZZ IN ROME, WWW.BUZZINROME.COM**

What to do, where to go, honest accounts of where to eat and current exhibitions.

**EMIKO DAVIES, WWW.EMIKODAVIES.COM**

A lovely blog about Italian cooking.

**KATIE PARLA, WWW.PARLAFOOD.COM**

Great, up-to-date and honest advice and an app to buy for latest restaurants and things going on.

# Index

# Bibliography

**AL DENTE BY DAVID WINNER, SIMON AND SCHUSTER, 2011**

Half David Winner's essays on Rome and half about its food, it is a strange and compelling read and one to keep dipping back into for more of his original thoughts on his adoptive city.

**THE CLASSICAL COOKBOOK BY ANDREW DALBY AND SALLY GRAINGER, BRITISH MUSEUM PRESS, 1996**

An eye-opening book about the historical cooking from ancient Greece and Rome.

**CUCINA ROMANA BY SARA MANUELLI, CONRAN OCTOPUS, 2005**

Written by Roman Sara, it is a lovely book full of clear recipes divided into the areas of Rome and accompanied by Lisa Linder's gorgeous photos.

**DELIZIA! BY JOHN DICKIE, SCEPTRE, 2007**

An enlightening account of the development of Italian food from Medieval Italy to the present day.

**FOOD, WINE, ROME BY DAVID DOWNIE, THE LITTLE BOOK ROOM, 2009**

A fascinating read about the areas and their well-established food stores and restaurants.

**ITALIAN REGIONAL COOKING BY ADA BONI, GODFREY CAVE, 1969**

A selection of 14 regions and their typical dishes with dated but wonderful photos. I love this book to help me step back in time – loads of inspiration for real and rustic cooking.

**LA CUCINA ROMANA E DEL LAZIO BY LIVIO JANNATTONI, NEWTON COMPTON EDITORI, 2013**

A massive book written in Italian, full of Roman recipes and their history, anecdotes and origins.

**LA MIA CUCINA, EBRAICO ROMANESCA BY BRUNA TEDESCHI, LOGART PRESS, 2009**

Written in Italian this specialises in recipes from the Jewish Roman tradition.

**MEMORIA A MOZZICHI BY ARCANGELO DANDINI AND BETTA BERTOZZI, GARGANTUA AND PANTAGRUEL, 2011**

Written in Italian by Dandini, one of the most famous Roman chefs whose passion for history and detail makes his food and recipes irresistible.

**THE OPERA OF BARTOLOMEO SCAPPI (1570) TRANSLATED BY TERENCE SCULLY, UTP, 2011**

Hundreds of recipes for how to cook dishes from the 1500s originally written by chef Scappi. This is the first English translation, which thankfully makes these wonderful recipes accessible to us all.

**THE OXFORD COMPANION TO ITALIAN FOOD BY GILLIAN RILEY, OXFORD, 2007**

A trustworthy and dependable source of information regarding chefs, ingredients and origins of recipes. We couldn't write about Italian food without it.

**ROMAN COOKERY BY MARK GRANT, ANCIENT RECIPES FOR MODERN KITCHENS, SERIF, 2008**

I'm so glad I found this inspirational book. It's a must for anyone interested in finding some really unusual recipes first created in Ancient Rome but that continue to taste amazing today.

**THE ROMAN COOKING OF APICIUS BY JOHN EDWARDS, RANDOM HOUSE, 1993**

A brilliant and easy to read translation of the 360 recipes originally written under the name of Apicius at the time of ancient Rome.

**ROME BY MAUREEN B. FANT/WELDON OWEN, BONNIER BOOKS, 2006**

Good, clear recipes, photographs and information about Roman food history and ingredients.

**THE TALISMAN ITALIAN COOK BOOK BY ADA BONI, PAN, 1950**

A huge variety of standard Italian recipes from all areas of Italy with simple recipes to follow. A mine of information and inspiration.

# About the Authors

Owners of London's Caldesi in Marylebone, Caldesi in Campagna in Bray, and the Marylebone La Cucina Caldesi cooking school, Katie and Giancarlo Caldesi have a passion for Italian food. They have spent over 25 years teaching students at every level, and have written 17 cookbooks. Katie and Giancarlo have two children, Giorgio and Flavio.

First edition (*Rome*) published in 2015 by Hardie Grant Books.

This edition published in 2023 by Hardie Grant Books,
an imprint of Hardie Grant Publishing

Hardie Grant Books (London)
5th & 6th Floors
52-54 Southwark Street
London SE1 1UN

Hardie Grant Books (Melbourne)
Ground Floor, Building 1
658 Church Street
Melbourne, VIC 3121

www.hardiegrantbooks.com

British Library Cataloguing-in-Publication Data. A catalogue record
for this book is available from the British Library.

Recipes from Rome
ISBN: 978-1-78488-628-8

10 9 8 7 6 5 4 3 2 1

Publishing Director: Kajal Mistry
Acting Publishing Director: Emma Hopkin
Commissioning Editor: Kate Burkett
Photographer: Helen Cathcart
Design + Illustration: A+B Studio (Amelia Leuzzi + Bonnie Eichelberger)
Copy Editor: Susan Pegg
Proofreader: Kate Wanwimolruk and Helen Graves
Indexer: Cathy Heath

Colour Reproduction by p2d
Printed and bound in China by Leo Paper Products Ltd.